3 463

D1188593

the series on school reform

Patricia A. Wasley	Ann Lieberman	Joseph P. McDonald
University of Washington	NCREST	New York University

SERIES EDITORS

(Continued)

This series also incorporates earlier titles in the Professional Development and Practice Series

Guiding School Change

The Role and Work of Change Agents

FRANCES O'CONNELL RUST
HELEN FREIDUS

EDITORS

Teachers College, Columbia University
New York and London

Published by Teachers College Press, 1234 Amsterdam Avenue, New York, NY 10027

Library of Congress Cataloging-in-Publication Data

Guiding school change : the role and work of change agents / Frances O'Connell Rust, Helen Freidus, editors.
    p. cm. — (The series on school reform)
   Includes bibliographical references and index.
   ISBN 0-8077-4115-9 (cloth) — ISBN 0-8077-4114-0 (pbk.)
    1. Educational change. 2. School management and organization. I. Rust, Frances O'Connell. II. Freidus, Helen. III. Series.
LB2805 .G83 2001
371.2—dc21   2001016203

ISBN 0-8077-4114-0 (paper)
ISBN 0-8077-4115-9 (cloth)

Printed on acid-free paper
Manufactured in the United States of America

08 07 06 05 04 03 02 01   8 7 6 5 4 3 2 1

Contents

Chapter 8
**The Professional Lives of Change Agents: What They Do
and What They Know**
ANN LIEBERMAN

Epilogue
Odyssey of a Coach (In Process)
CHARLOTTE LAK

Guiding School Change

The Role and Work
of Change Agents

Introduction

Frances O'Connell Rust and Helen Freidus

> *Rationalists wearing square hats,*
> *Think in square rooms,*
> *Looking at the floor,*
> *Looking at the ceiling.*
> *They confine themselves to right-angled triangles.*
> *If they tried rhomboids,*
> *Cones, waving lines, ellipses—*
> *As, for example, the ellipse of the half-moon—*
> *Rationalists would wear sombreros.*
>
> Wallace Stevens (1971)

For a very long time, it was believed that there were people who knew the answers to the problems of schools. These people, like Stevens's rationalists, conducted research in their laboratories, shared their findings, and "gave" professional developers the information and the tools they needed to make change (Kennedy, 1999). The only problem was that change did not occur. Too many children failed to learn. And so, teachers were blamed for not listening carefully, for not implementing instructional strategies systematically, and for not working hard enough. "If only teachers would follow these practices," the rationalists said, "children would learn."

Within this rationalistic perspective, cognition has been viewed as an individual function, and learning has been seen as the acquisition of knowledge and skills through the manipulation of thoughts and symbols *inside* the mind of the individual. Thus change is seen as the introduction, even imposition, of new models within and upon a system, and the process is understood to be driven by outside expertise. Typically, a change agent—more often than not a male—comes into a school system for a short period of time, a few months to a year or two. The expert transfers knowledge by modeling and disseminating "state-of-the-art" educational innovations. In this context teachers receive training, ask questions only for clarification, and—in the best of circumstances—dutifully apply the innovation to their classrooms as long as the expert and funds are available.

When funding and outside support end, most teachers continue using only those parts of the innovation that are closest to their prior practices. Ultimately, all but the nomenclature of the innovation fades. Thus the old patterns and structures persist: There has been little change in teachers' perceptions of themselves and their roles, minimal internalization of the concepts underlying the targeted change, and no organic change to the school, its discourse or its structures.

With the publication of the Rand Study on educational change (Berman & McLaughlin, 1978), a new school of thought began to emerge. Berman and McLaughlin demonstrated that change implementations were most successfully institutionalized when inside personnel were given time and authority to work alongside of outside change agents, when they were able to assume increasing responsibility for the change, and when teachers were provided with ongoing support after the change agent had left the district.

New ways of understanding cognition and the learning processes that are related to it have emerged in recent research (Putnam & Borko, 2000; Rogoff, 1990). In these studies cognition and learning are understood as being (a) situated in particular physical and social contexts, (b) social in nature, and (c) distributed among participating individuals. Knowledge and the valued ways of expressing this knowledge are produced and shaped within the context of "discourse communities." For teachers, schools are the primary discourse communities. As Hargreaves (1996) points out, "One's teaching, what one knows about teaching, and what one believes is possible and desirable in one's teaching all vary according to the context in which the teaching is done" (p. 15).

From this perspective, learning is envisioned as a process of social construction. If one extends this perspective on learning to the arena of professional development, past and present experiences of the individual and of the group as a whole can be seen as foundational to new understandings. As Dewey (1938/1963) writes, "Every experience lives on in future experiences" (p. 27). The history of an institution and the individuals within it inevitably shape the trajectory of a change implementation. Thus it becomes less important to ask about what teachers know than to observe and explore what they can think and do at particular times in particular contexts (Putnam & Borko, 2000). Seen in this light, successful change efforts are those that emerge from needs that are locally identified, appropriate to the specific context, and transformative for both individuals and institutions.

Following on the Rand Study, research on educational change conducted over the past decade identifies a set of conditions that strongly correlate with successful change efforts (Cochran-Smith & Lytle, 1993; Fullan, 1997; Fullan & Hargreaves, 1996; Hargreaves, 1992; Lieberman, 1995; McLaughlin, 1991):

- Collaborative cultures that foster professional learning communities
- Instructional practices that are relevant to and fully understood by teachers and students alike
- Instruction that is linked to the needs of individual students as well as the standards of the external community

Identification of these conditions, however, has not been enough to ensure successful change. Innovative structures, research tells us, are profoundly shaped by the interpersonal processes that accompany and surround them (Cochran-Smith & Lytle, 1993; Fullan & Hargreaves, 1996; Hargreaves & Fullan, 1998; Lieberman, 1995; McLaughlin, 1991). The success of reform efforts in schools is contingent upon effective collaboration over time (Hargreaves, 1996; Loucks-Horsely & Stiegelbauer, 1991). However, collaboration does not just happen. Facilitation is essential to the process. Who become the facilitators, the nature of their beliefs and experiences, their voices and their willingness to use these voices, and their knowledge of how adults learn and how groups work are now recognized as critical factors in reform. Thus it stands to reason that the preparation and support of those who take on the mantle of facilitator in a change initiative need to be better understood and articulated.

This book addresses the complexity of the facilitator's role by focusing on reform efforts as viewed through the lens of those who lead them—change agents. Our intent is to highlight their critical role and to draw attention to what we see as a serious oversight in the reform literature; namely how to prepare and support change agents throughout the change process. To do this, we have included the experiences of change agents across a broad range of contexts and have provided specific examples of what helped and impeded them in the roles with which they were charged.

NARRATIVES OF CHANGE

The chapters that follow document seven distinct but ideologically related change initiatives. In each of these, the work of change agents
proves to be dynamic, complex, and multidimensional. Whether the
change agents are insiders or outsiders, whether they work as guides,
mentors, facilitators, liaisons, tutors, or instructional supervisors, they
shape and are shaped by the context in which they work. Over the
course of time, their roles blend with the roles of others so that the
change process becomes a coconstruction between insiders and outsiders. In collaboration with one another, each participant

- brings his or her unique expertise to the process,
- learns with and from others, and
- engages in identifying ways to meet the needs of the children and
  adults in the setting.

Each of the chapters in this volume is written with a focus on the roles
and work of change agents. Each documents tensions that are simultaneously context specific and broad based. Each raises questions that
have significant implications for the field.

Chapter 1, by Rust, Ely, Krasnow, and Miller, reports on the professional development of teachers in Head Start and early elementary
grades in New York City. In this chapter the change agents are outsiders entering settings that have managed to maintain their status quo by
the co-optation of a long series of change initiatives. A critical question
emerges from this study: How—within a context of extreme poverty
and numbing bureaucracy—can the kind of caring essential for engen-
dering transformational change be provided and sustained?

Cynthia McCallister in Chapter 2 describes her experiences attempting to implement a schoolwide literacy change. She uses the metaphor of doors locked from within to represent the challenges an outsider faces in trying to influence core practices of schooling. The key
question raised by her work is this: How can a professional developer
come to understand and deal with the feelings of emotional pressure
and assault frequently encountered when working to implement meaningful change within schools whose cultures differ from her own?

In Chapter 3, Freidus, Grose, and MacNamara also look at efforts
to make curriculum change in the area of literacy. Their research focuses on professional developers who are insiders committed to change
at both the school and district levels. They describe a caring but results-
oriented environment in which high-stakes testing and new learn-

ing standards drive curriculum and instruction. How, they ask, in contexts like these, can professional developers seize time to craft the structures and pedagogies needed for teachers to be responsive to all learners?

Working on the West Coast, Kim Grose in Chapter 4 describes the work of Americorps interns working as partners-in-change with teachers in Bay Area schools. The professional developers she describes are college graduates who come with commitment to, but limited experience in, the specific processes of educational change. She describes them as both insiders and outsiders—working 4 days a week in the schools, they spend 1 day engaged in their own professional development. This chapter shows how these young people contribute to the reform process but raises questions about the tensions and constraints inherent in the work of change agents whose tenure within the school community is limited to 2-year intervals.

In Chapter 5, Snyder and D'Emidio-Caston describe the impact of state-mandated changes on a university-based program of teacher education. They look at the ways in which the supervisory experience serves as a form of professional development for preservice faculty and the teachers they serve. They ask, How do the prior knowledge and experience of teachers influence their visions of teacher education and their responses to professional development?

Cheryl Craig's account of a funded project in a large city reveals the tensions faced by a professional developer working to establish reform in a prereform city. Chapter 6 documents her struggle to establish collaborative processes within highly bureaucratized educational structures that serve large numbers of children in poverty. This chapter frames the question, What understandings and skills make up the tool kit needed if an outside change agent is to effect and support change within a resistant culture?

In Chapter 7, Ershler Richert, Stoddard, and Kass focus on the complexity of partnership work and how it can be supported for the purpose of widespread school change. The partners in this case are each comprised of subpartnerships between school districts and institutions of higher education. Addressing their own initiatives, they come together under the aegis of the Bay Area School Reform Collaborative to leverage educational reform throughout the region. The question that emerges from their work is this: How can a collaboration of individual initiatives effect systemic change throughout a region?

Ann Lieberman in Chapter 8 provides a succinct summary of research relevant to the work of change agents, and shows us how these narratives fit within and expand understandings of this important line of inquiry. The cases described here provide the human dimension to an important aspect of the research on change.

DEFINING THE ROLE OF CHANGE AGENT

What emerges from the narratives in this volume is a clearer picture than was available before of the personal side of change. Particularly important are the multiple roles that change agents assume and the complex interactions in which they participate. We can extrapolate from these accounts to highlight here four critical roles of change agents: negotiators, nurturers, teachers and learners, and curriculum developers.

Change Agents as Negotiators

Each setting evokes House's (1981, 1997) description of change as a negotiated process. Each focuses on a reform effort that brought together a range of stakeholders representing diverse perspectives and conflicting interests grounded in different or shifting paradigms. Change agents found themselves becoming negotiators in order to make the collaborative process work. Each had to develop a set of strategies and skills for working effectively with individuals and groups to help them identify their needs. Each had to construct a plan of action. Each had to learn to work together with other participants over time.

Central to the learning of all of these change agents was an understanding that there are costs in change for each stakeholder (House, 1997). Successful collaboration, as these studies show, involves participants' becoming aware of these costs and developing ways to reframe them as assets. Successful collaboration, they learned, inevitably involves ongoing redefinition of power structures. Who will guide the collaboration, what the process will look like, what outcomes will be accomplished in what time frame—all are salient issues that need to be discussed rather than mandated.

Change Agents as Nurturers

Across these chapters, the most successful interactions described are those that are experiential and dialogical. In these accounts, everyone is at some point or another a learner, and everyone has need for support. The conditions for learning are not new, but in the context of educational reform they seem surprising. Too often in the process of change, we have neglected the personal and interpersonal factors that contribute to the motivation to learn and the willingness to explore new ideas and new ways of being. First among these is trust, the sense that the relationship between knower and learner is solid, dependable, and honest. Together these narratives show that trust is commonly taken as a given rather than as a relationship that must be developed and redeveloped as the change process evolves.

In these stories, autobiography figured strongly. Change agents drew deeply from the well of their personal experience and from their understandings of adult learning. They drew on their prior experience as teachers and staff developers, and, in some cases, on their experience as parents. They drew on their own ways of knowing, their own understandings of family and community, and they used these as a point of departure to help them make sense of and appropriately respond to the demands of their settings.

Change Agents as Teachers and Learners

These change agents were teachers, but teachers of adults, not children. They learned to see themselves and the adults with whom they worked as learners. They came to see that adults construct new knowledge not by simple acquisition of skills and practices but by the process of drawing on prior understandings to make sense of the world. Thus these change agents needed to find both time and ways to guide new practice. They also came to see that there are stages through which adults develop and to appreciate that for adults, just as for children, there are enormous variations within these stages (Loevinger, 1976; Kegan, 1982). They came to recognize that adults in the same context with apparently similar experience and backgrounds may respond to new experiences in different ways. And they came to see that awareness of these differences is essential to initiating and sustaining innovations.

These change agents were teachers who clearly saw their task as motivators, facilitators, and organizers, but they had to learn the delicate balance of guiding and letting go so that others could take on these tasks. This was their central learning and their hardest task. As these accounts make clear, most had little or no support for this aspect of their work.

Change Agents as Curriculum Developers

In each of the reform efforts described here, change agents either introduced a new mode of instruction or worked with teachers to reshape their classroom practice. Each initiative was shaped by a belief in the value of a learner-centered, inquiry approach to education. Thus each change agent was engaged in developing strategies and skills that enabled teachers and administrators to experience and incorporate not only instructional methods that were in synchrony with the innovation but also habits of mind that would ensure the longevity of the innovation. This required both a deep understanding of the innovation and the skill to communicate this understanding in ways that provided a schematic sense of how the innovation could unfold and be institutionalized as well as a supportive scaffolding for those who would use it.

TENSIONS AND OBSTACLES

As Ann Lieberman points out in Chapter 8, the contributors to this volume identify obstacles and tensions that are critical both to the work of change agents and the change process itself. While many of these obstacles, as Lieberman makes clear, have been previously identified, some, particularly those having to do with the interpersonal aspects of the change process, have been minimized, even overlooked, in the research on professional development and school reform.

In some of the initiatives described in this book, tensions emerged when the goals of funders and administrators looking for immediate results conflicted with the goals of teachers and professional developers invested in the long-term process of aligning beliefs with action (see Chapters 1 and 6). In others, tensions emerged because the benchmarks for measuring success were not consonant with the philosophy and practice of the implementation (see Chapters 3 and 7). These tensions and obstacles appear to be related to issues of power and control, measurement of success, and the need for ongoing support over time.

Issues of Power and Control

The change agents in these initiatives found that some administrators voiced a commitment to a change implementation without fully understanding its implications. Motivated by desires to be on the cutting edge of reform, to take advantage of funding opportunities, and to be politically correct, they seemed to feel that every offering should be accepted. Inevitably this sort of myopia led to tension, even hostility, between change agents and administrators. As change agents tried to help teachers to change their paradigms, some administrators held on to beliefs in hierarchical structures. They paid lip service to the targeted innovation while they simultaneously promoted classroom practices that vied with its philosophical underpinnings. In these circumstances, change agents found themselves caught in the middle, lacking the authority that would enable them to effectively support the changes they championed. This was evident in some of the schools in which Freidus, Grose, and McNamara (Chapter 3) documented the implementation of reading initiatives and those in which Craig (Chapter 6) guided systemic reform efforts.

In other cases, the change agents themselves had difficulty recognizing and accepting alternatives to traditional lines of authority. For these individuals, helping others to look at structures in new ways was a daunting task; they themselves were unable to see beyond the status quo. This was the case for one of the supervisor-mentors described by Synder and D'Emidio-Caston in Chapter 5. Being an insider was part of the problem. With no regular interaction with other school cultures that might provoke questioning and reflection, she drew only on her own experience. In contrast, the other supervisor, facing similar problems but coming from outside of the field in the role of graduate student, was able to interact in ways that showed that she could adopt different lenses for addressing critical issues.

Measurement of Success

Who determines the criteria of successful teaching? What happens when the benchmarks of success are not consonant with the immediate goals of the change implementation? Such questions are becoming increasingly important in discussions of reform as the nation places a new emphasis on accountability. Each of these concerns has been relevant to the work described in these chapters.

Despite convincing research to the contrary (Darling-Hammond, 1997, 1998; Fullan, 1997), school boards, school administrators, and politicians continue to measure educational success through test scores and checklists. These may reflect an innovation's surface impact on performance, but they cannot provide indication of the innovation's impact on teaching and learning. What is needed are multiple measures of progress gathered systematically over time, like those that figure in the Head Start study conducted by Rust, Ely, Krasnow, and Miller (Chapter 1) and in the Bay Area School Reform Project conducted by Ershler Richert, Stoddard, and Kass (Chapter 7). However, as these two accounts demonstrate, portraits of an innovation's success vary according to the ways in which competing goals are addressed and interpreted.

Insufficient or Inappropriate Support

Just as the research on teaching shows that what happens in the class-room at the beginning of the year becomes a predictor for what will follow, the time and support invested in the early stages of a school reform effort are reflected in its outcomes (Darling-Hammond, 1997; Hargreaves, 1994; McLaughlin, 1991). What the narratives in this book show that has not been previously documented is that change agents not only need to give time and support, they need to receive it as well.

In the initiative described in Chapter 3, change agents recognized the importance of building trust with their teachers, but found their efforts severely compromised by their own lack of trust. As pointed out in Chapter 1, the early stages, really the first year, were critical for establishing trust and common goals. And the innovation analyzed in Chapter 2 showed that the failure to follow through on initial efforts to calibrate support in appropriate ways throughout the course of the effort may seriously compromise its implementation. Together, the chapters in this volume provide overwhelming evidence that for learning and the reshaping of priorities to be ongoing, support must be available not just in the beginning but on an ongoing basis and not just for teachers but for all participants.

LESSONS

We are just beginning to understand that change agents who work with teachers and administrators to guide them through change are also go-ing through a process of growth and development themselves (Freidus, Grose, & McNamara, 1996; Rust, 1993). Frequently the process of change pushes them into a state of disequilibrium which in turn influ-ences the roles they play and the ways in which they perceive and are perceived by those with whom they work. They too need time and sup-port that should be provided not just in initial training sessions but on an ongoing basis.

Supporting Change Agents

The change agents in these studies had had little experience with the demands of the new roles in which they found themselves. They often experienced doubt and anxiety about their own skills and under-standings. Like the teachers with whom they worked most closely, they too needed help in identifying and extending their own knowledge and skills. Like the teachers, they felt more successful when they experienced a sense of agency, when they found connections between the innovation and their own experience, and when they were able to adapt a reform in ways that made it valuable for those with whom they were working (Berman & McLaughlin, 1978; Cuban, 1988; McLaughlin, 1991).

Valuing Both Insider and Outsider Knowledge

Also emerging as critical in each of these accounts is the recognition and valuing of the funds of knowledge that each of the stakeholders brings to the exchange. Some change efforts described here were initiated by insiders: teachers, administrators, and parents. Some were initiated by outsiders: foundations and business partners. Some were mandated by outside agencies. That change agents as outsiders brought to these settings specific areas of expertise and specific tools emerging from research and practice is incontestable. These areas constituted essential knowledge in the implementation of the various reform initiatives that were studied. However, this expertise was balanced and nuanced by the specific contexts in which these initiatives took place and by the areas of expertise of insiders.

The process of facilitating change, as these accounts so powerfully demonstrate, is in itself a form of discovery learning whereby new understandings are shaped by the interchange of inside and outside, and by old and new experiences and habits of mind. The growth and development of all participants became essential to the change process. Knowing and learning were everyone's work, work that was mutually directed toward reform. Insiders knew what had been successful in the past and what had failed. They held the keys to the core beliefs and practices with which all new information would have to be integrated. The expertise that outsiders brought to the reform effort often became a catalyst, activating and extending insiders' funds of knowledge, their particular strengths, and their intimate knowledge of their own institutions.

In this process, partnerships formed in which roles appeared to blur. In other cases, insiders gradually assumed increasing responsibility for the implementation of transactional, inquiry-oriented modes of teaching. In other cases, outsiders gradually came to be perceived as insiders with new understandings of institutional history and culture that enabled them to garner trust and work effectively within the structures and values of the community.

Building Understandings

In these initiatives, understandings shifted as the change process un-
folded. This was as true for the change agents as it was for those with
whom they worked.

Regardless of how they began, the process of coming together was
more difficult, more stressful, and more uncertain than anyone had anticipated. These change agents were, we think, typical in that they entered the reform process believing that they understood what their roles
would be. They found, however, that these roles were constantly being
redefined. They rarely anticipated how much of their role would involve negotiation. They frequently underestimated the ways in which
context would influence their work.

They did not expect the tensions that would emerge around language—because a common language does not imply shared meanings—
and around assumptions about the relationships between change agents
and the communities with which they work—for example, that the
change agent could be and should be in harmony with all of the stakeholders in an innovation. Thus Cheryl Craig (Chapter 6) had to learn
how to articulate the message of constructivist practice both to administrators who were worried about the reputation of their schools in a
climate of high-stakes testing and to teachers who were feeling the pressure of the tests. The site facilitators in the work described by Rust,
Ely, Krasnow, and Miller (Chapter 1) had to engage in a similar task,
but among early childhood educators who thought that they were already engaged in learner-centered practice. This form of collaborative
process impacts on the participants in ways that are both personal and
professional (Hargreaves, 1994), and as these studies demonstrate, this
is rarely considered as part of the preparation or on-going support of
change agents.

Challenged by the complex demands of the change effort in their
various settings, the change agents came to recognize that they did not
have all the answers. They learned that both insiders and outsiders
need a repertoire of strategies and skills. However, change agents also
need to feel empowered to modify these in ways that are most effective
for identifying and meeting the conflicting needs of the stakeholders.
Change agents in these studies found that in order to be successful,
they needed to facilitate experiences and interactions that would lead
all participants, including themselves, to new constructions of knowledge. Each needs, as Lak's poem suggests (Epilogue), "a coach in process."

CONCLUSION

The picture of change that emerges in this book is one in which teams of people deeply committed to their work, their institutions, and their craft come together to shape and guide the reform efforts. This process stands in contrast to past models of change wherein new information was disseminated and superimposed upon, but not necessarily integrated with, teachers' and administrators' prior knowledge and experience.

It is our hope that these narratives will serve multiple functions: (1) giving substance to the personal and interactive nature of change, (2) helping the reader to identify ways in which effective change involves a process of negotiation among all stakeholders, and (3) demonstrating that successful change engages all participants in a process of growing and learning that requires ongoing support. These accounts show common understandings and points of view can emerge in this process when opportunities are made for participants to share the perspectives they bring and the perspectives they are building. Those who guide the change process bear the responsibility for creating these opportunities and encouraging and mediating the articulation of diverse perspectives within them (Moll, 1997).

We are now facing unprecedented challenges and opportunities in the arena of school reform. The growth and diversity of urban schools, the increasing number of children living in poverty with its concomitant stresses on families, schools, and communities, the projected aging-out of the majority of the teaching force, and the realignment of support for public education—these are only a few of the issues facing educators at this moment. While they present tremendous challenges, they also hold tremendous opportunity for rethinking, reshaping, and re-visioning schools and schooling. For this work, the narratives and analyses that follow have much to teach us about what makes a difference over time for children, their teachers, and their schools.

REFERENCES

Berman, P. B., & McLaughlin, M. W. (1978). *Implementing and sustaining innovations*. Vol. 8 of *Federal programs supporting educational change* (Rand Report No. R-1589/8-HEW). Santa Monica, CA: Rand.
Cochran-Smith, M., & Lytle, S. (Eds.) (1993). *Inside/Outside: Teacher research and knowledge*. New York: Teachers College Press.

Cuban, L. (1988). A fundamental puzzle of school reform. *Phi Delta Kappan*, 70(5), 341–344.

Darling-Hammond, L. (1997). *The right to learn*. San Francisco: Jossey-Bass.

Darling-Hammond, L. (1998). Teachers and teaching: Testing policy hypotheses from a national commission report. *Educational Researcher*, 27(1), 5–15.

Dewey, J. (1963). *Experience and Education*. New York: Macmillan. (Original work published 1938)

Freidus, H., Grose, C., & McNamara, M. (1996). *Something old, something new: Issues arising from the implementation of a holistic literacy program within an urban school system*. Paper presented at the annual meeting of the National Reading Conference, Scottsdale, Arizona.

Fullan, M. (1997). Emotion, and hope: Constructive concepts for complex times. In A. Hargreaves (Ed.), *Rethinking educational change with heart and mind. 1997 ASCD Yearbook* (pp. 216–233). Alexandria, VA: Association for Supervision and Curriculum Development (ASCD).

Fullan, M., & Hargreaves, A. (1996). *What's worth fighting for in your school?* New York: Teachers College Press.

Hargreaves, A. (1992). Cultures of teaching: A focus for change. In A. Hargreaves & M. Fullan (Eds.), *Understanding teacher development* (pp. 216–240). New York: Teachers College Press.

Hargreaves, A. (1994). *Changing teachers, changing times: Teachers' work and culture in the postmodern age*. New York: Teachers College Press.

Hargreaves, A. (1996). Revisiting voice. *Educational Researcher*, 25(1), 12–19.

Hargreaves, A., & Fullan, M. (1998). *What's worth fighting for out there?* New York: Teachers College Press.

House, E. A. (1981). Three perspectives on innovation: Technological, political, cultural. In R. Lehming & M. Kane (Eds.), *Improving schools: Using what we know* (pp. 17–41). Beverly Hills, CA: Sage.

House, E. A. (1997). A framework for appraising educational reforms. *Educational Researcher*, 25(7), 6–14.

Kegan, R. (1982). *The evolving self*. Cambridge, MA: Harvard University Press.

Kennedy, M. (1999). A test of some common contentions about educational research. *American Educational Research Journal*, 36(3), 511–541.

Lieberman, A. (Ed.). (1995). *The work of restructuring schools: Building from the ground up*. New York: Teachers College Press.

Loevinger, J. (1976). *Ego development*. San Francisco: Jossey-Bass.

Loucks-Horsely, S., & Stiegelbauer, S. (1991). Using knowledge of change to guide staff development. In A. Lieberman & L. Miller (Eds.), *Staff development for education in the '90s* (pp. 15–36). New York: Teachers College Press.

McLaughlin, M. W. (1991). Enabling professional development: What have we learned? In A. Lieberman & L. Miller (Eds.), *Staff development for education in the '90s* (pp. 61–82). New York: Teachers College Press.

Moll, L. (1997). *The creation of mediating settings: Mind, culture and activity*.

Los Angeles: Regents of the University of California on behalf of the Laboratory of Comparative Human Cognition.

Putmam, R., & Borko, H. (2000). What do new views of knowledge and thinking have to say about research on teacher learning? *Educational Researcher, 29*(1), 4–15.

Rogoff, B. (1990). *Apprenticeship in thinking: Cognitive development in social context.* New York: Oxford University Press.

Rust, F. O'C. (1993). *Changing teaching, changing schools: Bringing early childhood practice into elementary schools.* New York: Teachers College Press.

Stevens, W. (1990). Six significant landscapes. In H. Stevens (Ed.), *The palm at the end of the mind* (pp. 15–17). New York: Vintage.

Professional Development of Change Agents: Swimming With and Against the Currents

Frances O'Connell Rust, Margot Ely,
Maris H. Krasnow, and LaMar P. Miller

What are the dynamics of change for those who guide the process in the field? Current research includes extensive discussion of the role of professional development in the process of changing practice in educational settings. It describes how change must be adopted, not imposed (McLaughlin, 1993); how change is complex and must be understood as such (Fullan, 1993; Sarason, 1990); and how change takes place over time (Fullan 1993, 1997). It is well documented that if change is to be effective, attention must be paid to teachers' voices (Lieberman, 1988); their concerns, beliefs, and experiences (Fuller, 1969); and the ways in which personal and professional funds of knowledge intersect and play out in the classroom context (Clandinin & Connelly, 1995; Cochran-Smith, 1995; Cochran-Smith & Lytle, 1993; Loucks-Horseley & Stiegelbauer, 1991). Little attention, however, has been paid to the process of personal and professional change that is experienced by professional developers themselves (Freidus, 1996; Rust, 1989).

In this chapter, we explore the ways in which the process of assuming the role of professional developer is in itself a change process. It is complex; it takes time; it is affected by context; and it involves the shaping and reshaping of the personal and professional landscapes of those involved. Here, we focus on the work of four site facilitators over the course of a 5-year collaboration (1993–1998) between a foundation, a major university, and four Head Start centers that aimed to effect changes in teaching practice in early childhood classrooms.

The project, Teaching for Success, was conceived as a site-sensitive staff development project that combined what we considered the best of developmentally appropriate, learner-centered instruction with current knowledge about the process of change and professional development. Essential to the institutionalization of this initiative in the centers was the interactive support work of four site facilitators as they interpreted and implemented the project's methods and goals in ways that incorporated both their own lived experience as teachers and their understandings of the settings within which they were working.

We used qualitative research methods to describe and understand the dynamics of change. In order to generate layers of data that best capture the complexity of the project (Lincoln & Guba, 1985), this study drew on researcher journals, site facilitators' logs, open-ended interviews, audiotaped focus group discussions, and videotapes of classroom interactions. Data collection and analysis was guided by a recursive, comparative process (Lincoln & Guba, 1985) designed to inform our understanding of the intersection of personal development, professional development, and context in the change process. What emerged is a story that has helped us understand the process of change in ways that we could not have predicted at the outset. We have chosen to tell this story from the site facilitators' perspectives since it was their interpretations of their roles, more than any other factor, that shaped the process and outcomes of this change effort.

PROJECT DESIGN

Teaching for Success was designed as a 4-year staff development project for four Head Start centers in New York City, although a 5th year was negotiated among the various participants in the spring of 1997 to allow for networking among the centers and to extend support for one center that joined the project a year later than the others. The centers were selected by the Robin Hood Foundation as sites where substantive work in staff development might take place. And we—Rust, Ely, and Miller (faculty at New York University)—were asked by the Foundation to develop a staff development plan that could result in significant and sustained systemic change in the centers.

Before we shaped our plan, we went to visit each center. Our implicit assumption then, as now, was that the change process is contextually sensitive: In each setting, it would look and feel different. What we needed to determine, therefore, were the particular strengths and needs of each of the four sites and the areas of overlap among them. We saw our task as shaping and implementing a staff development plan that was internally consistent in that the same goals and the same elements would be present at every site, but would be articulated through site-based personnel (our site facilitators) in ways that were consistent with the culture of each center.

From the outset our work was guided by questions about the transformation of practice in the Head Start centers and in the public schools that received their students. Specifically, we focused on the process of change within and across the centers and the schools, the impact of the staff development program on the practice of the Head Start and public school teachers involved, and changes in children's performance over time. Thus our 4-year plan, while not quite the "ready, fire, aim" approach that Fullan (1993) describes, was by virtue of the circumstances a general approximation of what we hoped would happen in the time allotted.

We limited our intervention to the nine full-day classes in the four centers. We reasoned that with their stable populations of children and teachers across the day, these classes would provide continuity for our work and might serve as critical points for dissemination of the project activities. Further, we concluded that since the site facilitators' time was limited to 2½ days per week in the centers, and since they would work it would be possible for them to work effectively with no more that two or three classes in each center.

We saw Year 1 as the mobilization phase of the project, a time for us to get to know one another and develop trust. We knew that the quality of the relationships developed in that first year would be critical to the stability and longevity of our collaboration with the centers and with the foundation. Simultaneously, however, there was the pressure of time and vision. Hence Years 1 and 2 were also envisioned as the implementation phase of the project, the period in which the project would take shape. Year 3 was seen as the institutionalization phase, and Year 4 as a time for fine-tuning prior to the withdrawal of funds.

The program had three key components:

1. *Staff development.* We set out to support teachers and staff first in the Head Start centers and later in the public schools in implementing those early childhood teaching practices that research and experience have shown best support young children's cognitive, social, and emotional growth.
2. *Support of children's learning.* We sought to help teachers and

staff enhance the educational experience of the children with whom they work.

3. *Research and policy development.* We aimed to provide data to the Robin Hood Foundation that might guide policy and planning in early childhood education in both local and national forums.

To accomplish these goals we insisted on several program essentials:

- *A site facilitator in each center.* We chose four experienced early childhood teachers and matched each with a center.
- *A weekly hour-long team meeting of the faculty of the full-day classes in each center with their respective site facilitator.* No administrators were to be present. This was to be a time for teachers to focus entirely on their work with children and to share this discussion across the classes.
- *Monthly seminars at NYU.* Teachers, parent representatives, aides, and other staff in participating classrooms were to attend along with center administrators and educational directors.
- *A weekend retreat in the fall of each year.* Initially, we planned a retreat only for the first year. However, the participants' responses to the first retreat were so positive that we reshaped our plan and gradually moved the decision-making about the focus and implementation of each retreat to planning teams from each of the centers.
- *Ongoing formative assessment.* This would involve using videotaped analyses of classroom interactions, site facilitators' logs, child study data, and interviews with faculty, administrators, staff, and parents.
- *Yearly assessments of children's progress by an outside agency.* Philliber Research Associates would use the Child Observation Record (High/Scope, 1991).

In many ways, the project stayed remarkably true to this initial conceptualization. In other ways, however, it reminded us of how messy, uncertain, erratic, and open to unforeseen events is the process of change.

PROJECT MOBILIZATION

Choosing the On-Site Team

In April 1993, Maris Krasnow, at that time an adjunct faculty member in the Early Childhood and Elementary Education Program of the NYU

Department of Teaching and Learning, joined our team as the site coordinator of the project. We put an ad in the *New York Times* seeking
individuals interested in working as site facilitators in a new staff development project related to Head Start. The ad brought applications from
several dozen people. After interviewing 10, we chose 4: two New York
City elementary school teachers on sabbatical, Nancy and Harriet; a
former Head Start teacher now living in the suburbs, Jennifer; and a
former director of an early childhood lab school in a local college, Julie.
They said that they had been drawn to the project by the tone of the
ad and the possibility for professional growth. Their responses to it
gave us inklings about who they were and what they saw themselves
bringing to this work:

> It had my name written all over it. I mean, it was a job that I
> thought—not only can I do this but I would really enjoy doing
> this. (Jennifer)

> I certainly was an inner city school teacher and I had been a kin-
> dergarten teacher so I felt I was qualified for that, and I certainly
> worked with children, and the fact that it was NYU and it sound-
> ed like they were doing something very innovative. I was ready
> for that because things weren't too innovative where I was work-
> ing so that really caught my eye. (Harriet)

> It was an interesting ad and I thought that this is the kind of stuff
> that I want to be doing rather than spending my lifetime, I guess,
> fighting a system that wasn't going to change. (Nancy)

> [It was] a project you could sink your teeth into [and I] was very
> excited about people who are excited about working with young
> children. (Julie)

On the whole, we thought, "Here was a group of people who had
the requisite knowledge and experience, *and* they had heart!" We were
also impressed that none expressed concern about working in parts of
the city that are not considered "safe."

Quickly, we formed ourselves as a project team. We read and re-
read the proposal together. We brainstormed about how it might take
shape and evolve, and we made assignments to the full-day classes—
nine in all—at the four sites. The site facilitators were introduced to
the field.

Learning the Ropes

From the very beginning, the site facilitators drew on their prior experiences first in the ways that they responded to the ad and then in the shaping of their roles to be congruent with the overall philosophy of the project. We had been purposeful in our decision that how the facilitators worked had to be shaped by the contexts of the sites and by the individuals involved. Each was to function within the following set of parameters:

- Be in the centers 2½ days per week
- Be present at a weekly meeting held on-site with the team of teachers with whom each of them were working
- Attend the Head Start teachers' monthly seminars at NYU planned jointly by them and the rest of the team
- Attend a weekly project team meeting at NYU

Other than these activities, the site facilitators were supported in shaping their work in the centers as they deemed appropriate. And they exercised their prerogative.

The first months, really the first year, were simultaneously exciting, frustrating, energizing, heartbreaking, exhilarating, and, the site facilitators reported, the hardest work these four women had ever done. In retrospect, they still cannot agree on whether they should have had a clear job description. "You're not a staff developer. You're not a teacher. You're not a supervisor. It's a very anomalous position," Julie says. And Jennifer describes it as "seduction":

> Our job was much harder than just going in and cleaning house and fixing it. This I could do. Our job was to seduce and to win them over and cajole and please and pull and push and all the time trying to do it being nice with no power, with no budget.

Nancy describes the role as

> confusing at first. I didn't know what, what will I do? Don't do much. Just listen. I knew at first we had to build trust. It was a new role for me. In some ways difficult because in the past I had been able to do a lot, and that was a good thing; now, doing was not a good thing.

Defining Roles

We had anticipated that the first year would be a time of developing trust and understanding with the administrators, teachers, parents, and staff in the Head Start centers. We had not anticipated, however, the extent to which we, as the university-based team, would have to do this with the facilitators or they with us. Nor did we anticipate the level of stress that the facilitator's role might engender. Harriet described those early months in this way:

> I wasn't sure what the professors might want from me, what I should do if I . . . you know. I listened a lot. I was somewhat over-whelmed. I never worked that closely with college professors. I had always been in the role of student, and I had just finished my master's so I had been back in the college scene, but working on a collaborative basis, I thought that was very exciting. I thought it was a great way for me to learn and, yet, I was a little apprehensive.

What we all learned to do in our weekly meetings at NYU was to take time to listen to one another. We heard about the difficult situations that each of the facilitators was facing. We also heard about what we began to call "small victories": little changes like the appearance of labels on furniture, an alphabet list, a teacher taking the facilitator aside to ask a question. And these meetings became times for us to vent concerns and share our growing understandings of one another and the project.

We learned to give one another space, to trust the process and the structures that we had developed. Thus, feeling that they needed to debrief together and that there was a level of talk that the NYU team need not be involved in, site facilitators began meeting for lunch before they met with us.

> That was wonderful in terms of giving us a place to vent. Some-times we would show up for lunch, and there was always one of us that was like "wow" and we needed to just do that. Occasion-ally venting led to a certain amount of problem solving. It wasn't just venting but it was like well, here's what you might try or that kind of thing. But mostly I think it became just a kind of general bonding place. (Jennifer)

None of us was prepared for the emotional pull that the experience of working in close personal and professional quarters with teachers and administrators would have on us. What they and we quickly understood was that there were tremendous needs on the parts of both children and adults in each of the centers. As Jennifer put it,

> I don't think there was a single site facilitator who didn't at some moment just feel so overwhelmed emotionally because . . . certainly in some schools more than others . . . there was a tremendous amount of pain about seeing what was being done to children that was unbearable and what you wanted to do was just go in and fix it and then fire people.

But they couldn't fire people. They were bound by the terms of our grant to find ways to facilitate change. It was physically and emotionally exhausting.

Like new teachers, the site facilitators learned their limits. They learned to take time for themselves, they learned not to dwell on problems, and they learned to look to the small victories as signs of progress. Their logs grew thick with their growing perceptions of the centers and their work. Harriet began with worries about her ability to work with

> such young children: the 4-year-olds. I had experience with 5-year-olds, 4-and-a-half-year-olds, but these children were much younger. I wasn't sure what it would be like in a different agency, in a Head Start agency, although I was excited about Head Start because I had read so much about it so I was anxious to learn about the culture and the program.

She and the others quickly found that there was a general willingness on the part of the teachers to let them work, but that there was general distrust for them and the NYU team on the part of most of the administrators. Essentially, they were walking a veritable tightrope between the two groups.

In that first year, these women learned to draw deeply from the well of their experience as well as from the intangible reservoirs of good will and caring that grew between them, with the NYU team, and with some of the administrators and teachers in the centers. What each of them came to understand was that she was the key person in the project for her center. To their enormous surprise, each developed skills of collaborative leadership that fit the settings in which they found themselves.

THE LEADERSHIP OF THE CENTERS

While there were similarities among the centers—all, for example, served primarily Latino (Caribbean) families—and similarities in the work that each site facilitator was doing, there were also huge differences. Like any community of people, each center had its own unique character, which showed in the ways that they interpreted and responded to federal and local mandates, the ways that they were managed, and the ways that teachers, administrators, parents, and community members interacted over essential issues such as assessment.

The facilitators agreed that a critical factor in their work was the quality of the leadership in the center. Some learned to work with it and felt supported by it; others learned how to work around it.

Harriet worked with a very strong administrative team that was managing a multisite center. The director of her center, she says, "gave me the opportunity and she was smart because by empowering me, I could empower the teachers and they empowered the children. . . . I see that she has learned the power of empowering others." By its 4th year, Harriet's center had institutionalized much of the project throughout its five sites. Teachers in the first classrooms with which Harriet worked had taken on wider center leadership. Both our own assessments and those completed by Philliber Research Associates showed that the children in this center had become more active, engaged learners and were meeting with success in the elementary school programs to which they transferred after Head Start.

In contrast, Julie worked in a multisite center where the director was also very strong, though autocratic and authoritarian in her leadership style, and very much against the project. A woman totally dedicated to working with young children and families, Julie found the repressive atmosphere created by the center's administration the biggest hurdle in her work:

> It caused such disruption in teachers' emotional lives, too. Here they come, from us. They feel like they could do something, and then, bang, she just slams it down. She really did. It's like this ping-pong ball. It bounces up again, but, eventually, it bounces less and less.

Julie focused her energies on the teachers. Every step of the way seemed painfully slow to her.

> I didn't even see much change until the 2nd year and more change in the 3rd year because it is very slow and it's very stable and it

needs time to settle in. They need the support over time to become really grounded in this so they feel secure in what they're doing.

Nancy worked in a center where leadership was in a constant state of flux. Like Julie, she focused her attention on the teachers. She began in a way that was totally natural to her: She was approachable. She felt herself drawn into their lives and those of the families in her center. She said, "I had to be friendly with them but I had to get personal with them. . . . Before we could even get to what was going on in the classroom, we had to talk about what was happening at home." In this process of creating community, Nancy found that she was drawing a subtle curtain around her own personal life:

> I felt my life was very different from their lives and I didn't want to talk about my life because it was so different. I'm in such another world. It's like crossing over to this other world and I didn't want . . . I couldn't relate in that way.

Unlike so much of the story telling among people who are getting to know one another, Nancy's interactions with these teachers were not focused on establishing common ground so much as helping them shift and expand their vision:

> They have very hard lives. As soon as they start to pull themselves out from under it, they kind of defeat themselves. They want to go to school. They want to get a better job, and then, wooosh, they get pregnant so you can't do it. You just have to wait longer. It's like they're stuck in it, and I'm rooting for them all the time. Go take the class, go get the job, but it's like they're getting up and then, zoop, down. They have so many responsibilities, I can't even think about it, the individuals there with all the stresses in their lives and no support. It's difficult.

It was slow work. Even in the 4th year of the project, when the teachers in Nancy's center had in many ways transformed their classrooms and their practices, there was still a leadership vacuum that placed an extra burden on this group of teachers.

In the first 2 years, Jennifer worked in three of the four centers so she had a broad view of the context of the project. For the last 2 years, she was in a center where she described the power structure as being sort of diffuse. It's a funny sort of thing. There's no real leadership. The director is a powerful personality, but she doesn't really use her power, just lets it sort of erupt in little places. . . . It's like whoever is on top at the moment. You sort of try to figure out who's king of the hill at the moment. So, I don't think of it as top down or that it necessarily empowers people although I think there's a lot of potential there for it.

Thus Jennifer's work, like that of Nancy and Julie, was focused mainly on the teachers and on finding ways to help them shape a new vision for themselves as professionals.

PROJECT ASSESSMENT

Fundamental to the design of the project was ongoing assessment by the NYU team and by Philliber Research Associates, an outside evaluator contracted by the Robin Hood Foundation. It was our contention that the daily interaction of the site facilitators with teachers, administrators, children, and parents in the centers; the monthly seminars; and the annual retreats would have a substantial impact on teachers' interactions with children and thus on children's learning and behavior.

From the beginning, those aspects of the project that related to assessment were a source of difficulty for the site facilitators: They became the lightening rods for teachers' anxiety about being judged and for administrators' distrust of the project itself. For example, it took at least 4–6 months in several centers for the weekly meetings with the teachers to gain general acceptance as safe forums for teachers to engage in child study and to reflect on their work. In several of the centers, this sort of acceptance came well into the 2nd year.

Philliber Research Associates completed a yearly evaluation using the Child Observation Record (COR), which was developed by High/Scope (1991). The Child Observation Record focuses on six categories of behavior: initiative, social relations, creative representation, music and movement, language and literacy, and logic and mathematics. Once they had learned to use it, the teachers found that the instrument was extremely useful for identifying the skills and strengths of each child as well as for planning activities to meet specific children's needs. In the final year of the project when the teachers were working without the support of site facilitators, the COR data showed significant increases in every area across all of the centers. What they did not show was that the project teachers along with the site facilitators had taken the COR to other classrooms in their centers so that it had become an essential assessment tool for many teachers in each of the centers.

The NYU team used videotapes of classrooms as well as weekly observations by the site facilitators and bimonthly observations by the project coordinator and members of the team. After the first year, the videotapes were shared regularly with the teachers and were used for an intensive analysis of classroom interactions (see end reports to the Robin Hood Foundation: Ely, Miller, Rust, & Krasnow, 1994–1998; Philliber Research Associates, 1994–1998). Like the COR data, video analysis done over the 4 years showed a similar trend toward self-sufficiency on the part of the teachers and independent, self-initiated, and high-level cognitive activities on the part of the children. For the site facilitators, both the in-house and outside assessments provided irrefutable evidence of the impact of their work with the full-day teaching teams and their students and across those centers that embraced the project over time.

SUPPORT FOR SITE FACILITATORS

As they developed ways of interacting with teachers and administrators, learning to look for small victories, sharing these with the teachers, and getting the teachers to look at themselves, the site facilitators found support from one another, the weekly team meetings at NYU, and the project coordinator. As time went on, some of them found sources of support in their centers. The more experienced they became, the more they were able to see ways to draw on one another and on their prior experiences as teachers and facilitators to inform their practice in the centers.

Support from One Another

Although Harriet and Nancy did not know each other before the project began, their shared status as NYC elementary teachers on sabbatical provided an immediate link and enabled them to deliberate together about taking the job. Harriet said,

> [Nancy] had gone through this thing, this kind of work that I had in the inner-city schools, was disillusioned with the bureaucracy and all the other stuff that goes along with that and so, I said to myself, good, I've a nice partner here.

The bonding of the group took place, according to Julie,

> right from the beginning, I think there was a real passionate inter-
> est on the part of all of us, especially the facilitators, too. You felt
> that. Like Nancy and Harriet and Jennifer, they really cared about
> kids. It got me to be stronger as we went along, even when we
> had disagreements, whatever, that was always the foundation. We
> knew that they cared about the kids so right from the beginning
> there was a sense of colleagues in that respect or soul sisters or
> whatever you call it.

The relationship that these four women developed between them
was one of the strongest aspects of their support system. It was aug-
mented by the structure of the project itself and specifically the weekly
team meetings.

Support from the Project Structure

In some ways, these avenues of support were anticipated in our design
of the project. What we had not anticipated were ways in which the
regularities of the project itself became sources of support to the site
facilitators. For example, the site facilitators told us that the monthly
seminars with participants in which we worked initially on specific curriculum areas like math, block building, or language arts were "absolutely essential . . . because even if they didn't get something out of it,
it made it easier to start certain things going" (Julie). So, too, were the
weekly meetings that the facilitators held with the teachers. These became the special, trusting forums in which teachers and facilitators,
away from the watchful eye of administrators, could explore issues of
child study, classroom management, and professional development.

Weekly Team Meetings at NYU. We developed weekly team meetings
at the university as a way of enabling us to keep current with one another. For 2 hours each Wednesday afternoon, the site facilitators, project coordinator, and the NYU faculty met, planned, argued, listened,
laughed, and learned about the complexity of the work we had chosen
to undertake together. In their debriefing on the project, the site facilitators were unanimous in their identification of these meetings as a major
source of support and as a means of gaining understanding of the project. Julie described the meetings in this way:

> The weekly meetings were a lifeline because we could come with
> our concerns and talk about them especially the first year. It

seemed that we did a lot of griping and lot of . . . kind of storing your concerns until you got there and opened the bag and let it all out. This was where you could feel safe in expressing those concerns and get feedback from other people about how to deal with them the next time the situation ever came up. Just to air your concerns seemed to me to help a lot. Also, a sense of relief that other people are going through the same thing. You weren't the only one dealing with certain issues.

Annual Retreats. To start off the project, the entire NYU team, including the facilitators, planned a retreat for all the people involved in the project. We turned a Catskill resort into an early childhood center and set the teachers free to explore as we would want children to. That retreat helped to allay teachers', administrators', and facilitators' concerns about us, the NYU professors, and it established a bond of mutuality for our work together throughout the project.

I felt that the professors put themselves on a very equal basis with the on-site facilitators. We considered ourselves a team. It wasn't "we know more than you because we're the professors and you're the staff developers." I felt that my opinions were respected and I felt comfortable. Each group respected each other for what we had. I felt they respected me for my experiences. I think that did a lot to make it easier. (Harriet)

For the teachers, the first retreat was an extraordinarily powerful experience. They insisted on one each year after that and have become involved in planning and implementing these now annual events. Facilitators supported them in the planning. Julie's description is relevant:

The teachers loved the retreat because nobody was walking around with "I am so and so." We were all on a first name basis, and they really loved the idea of mingling with professors and with faculty. They felt like they are like a learning community and the teachers really remarked on it again and again. They really liked it.

Support from the Project Coordinator

Maris Krasnow, the project coordinator, was unquestionably a major source of support for the site facilitators as well as the hub of information about the project. She visited each center regularly. She knew all the players there—both the principals and minor ones. She was often on the phone with them. With the variety of information sources that she had at her disposal, she helped the site facilitators make sense of the things that they were experiencing and the problems that they were confronting.

> As site facilitators, we frequently felt like the middle of the sandwich so we had administrators, teachers, children, parents, whatever on the one side and what we were doing there which sometimes felt like we were doing that alone, isolated . . . Margot, Frances, LaMar, they sometimes felt like the other side. They were dealing with the overall and the abstract issues and the big picture, and you, Maris, were straddling both worlds and we watched you do that sometimes, going, my god, how is she doing that? So you were an important link for us. (Jennifer)

INSIGHTS

All of us learned a lot about the dynamics of change from our work in the centers. We became very sensitive to the issue of context and to the ways in which various project activities might be interpreted in the different centers.

> You have to ask yourself, "Is it me?" "Is it what I'm doing?" I've got my imperfections. I'm loud and I talk a lot, and I do all these things and in some places it works fine. . . . With some people, it's just fine and with other people, it's not so fine, and so you get some feedback. It's not only me. It isn't just that I'm an imperfect person. It's also context and knowing that some things are going to work and some things aren't going to work. (Jennifer)

We knew that change takes time. We had not appreciated its subtlety and the intensely personal quality of each individual's investment in the process. Julie describes it well:

> "You might want to take a look at this; you might want to try this and let me know what you think," I'd say. I learned that from here, too, from Maris. Maris said in the beginning that one way to do it was, for example, go into the block building and ask teachers to observe and comment on what we do so it's not threatening to them, teaching them that this is how you play but asking

them for their feedback. It's slow. Some of it was my past experience, I think, suggesting that some people have tried this and found it useful, you might want to look at it. So very, very low key . . . so the teachers see a difference, and when they see a difference and it works, it seems useful. It's still an issue of how much they're willing to invest in themselves because it is sometimes more work to meet the children and be prepared to do things. You have to be willing to put in that time. . . . You have to draw on the teacher's concerns as a starting point.

We did not appreciate at the beginning, maybe not fully even now, the precarious position that we were asking some teachers to occupy. In essence, we were supporting them to work toward more child-centered, teacher-empowered classrooms, while many of them were still members of highly codified, authoritarian settings. We knew that they would need skills and courage, and we were ready to provide the help and support that were necessary. But, we did not envision the frustration and pain that some of them would encounter as they tried to live into the classroom life that we had opened up to them. Julie describes it as "the law of unintended consequences: this smashup in the middle between teachers who now feel empowered and want to change and the top who won't let them, don't do enough about it to keep it going."

"You have to spark something that they want to change," Jennifer says. "It doesn't happen unless they want it to happen," says Julie. We discovered that teachers in a project like this have to be hopeful, to show a willingness to take risks, and to dream. And we learned that our visions of what might be had to give way to theirs. More surely than ever, we learned that there is no one right way, no orthodoxy beyond creating powerful, caring environments in which teachers and learners can purposefully interact. In the end, there is what works best for this teacher and these students at this time.

We had not appreciated how immensely difficult this work can be. Reflecting back on their 3 years of involvement, the site facilitators questioned how long a person can sustain a high level of involvement in such work:

I don't know if you could do this job of site facilitator for a long period of time without changing radically. . . . You want to do a job like this for 30 years, well, you'd need some major support, much more support than we put in place. You know, what we tried to set up for ourselves, would need to be restructured because of burnout. (Jennifer)

They also wondered whether and how things might be changing at the deepest layers. Were participants willing to confront the deep racial and social justice issues that are present in these settings? Were we? This was a question that none of us could answer.

PERSONAL CHANGE AND PROFESSIONAL GROWTH

Each of these women claims to have changed as a result of her involvement in this project. Each felt empowered to do more and achieve more than she had thought herself capable of when she began. Jennifer feels that she need not go on to graduate school:

> I feel like I've learned a tremendous amount about the group process, about facilitating, about the dynamics of power. At the beginning of this project, if you said, "plan, pick something up, a math workshop, a block workshop, whatever, for sixty people," I would have said, "No. I can't. I couldn't. I wouldn't know where to start." I don't feel that way anymore. I feel that I know . . . at least where to start. . . . I didn't know that I could do as much as I know now that I can do.

She has continued with her center as the on-site staff development coordinator, a position that did not exist before the Teaching for Success initiative.

Harriet has taken a position as an assistant principal in a high-powered school district. Nancy, who has returned to teaching first grade, is attracting widespread attention because of her insistence on parent involvement and because of her innovative curriculum. And Julie, completing a doctorate, starting an infant-toddler program, and continuing to work with teachers, is committed more than ever to learning, especially learning about how to improve the lives of children.

Each person can identify high points in her work—small victories that heralded substantive change in weeks, months, sometimes years to come. They leave this work knowing that they made a difference and that others will continue the process that they began.

CONCLUSION

We have seen that the work of change is highly personal and interactive and that it turns on the quality of professional support that is available not only for teachers (Garman, 1990; Gitlin & Price, 1992) but for professional developers as well. We found that with experienced teachers like our site facilitators, the process of developing expertise as facilitators of a change process followed a trajectory much like the "Stages of Concern about Innovation" outlined by Hall, Wallace, & Dorset (1973), but the process was both nonlinear and greatly foreshortened. In crafting their roles, our site facilitators gathered information, weighed the personal costs, and juggled concerns about management, consequences, and collaboration; but once they committed themselves to the project, it seemed as if they faced these concerns simultaneously and not in a step-by-step fashion. In the project's 3rd year as their roles were curtailed, they were forced to refocus, to think about next steps. This appears to be a different path and a much shorter time frame for moving through an innovation than the literature generally acknowledges. It reflects, we believe, the expertise and vision of the site facilitators on whom the project depended. It seems that it is evidence, as Gardner (1999) suggests about children's learning, that the ways in which learners, even adults, shape new understandings is by meshing new information and new insights with what they already know.

While the Hall et al. (1973) model is powerful for explaining some of the process followed by both professional development personnel spearheading an innovation and classroom teachers adopting the innovation, we believe that it does not take into account the subtle and very powerful shaping effect of personal autobiography. A major part of the initial learning of our site facilitators involved reflection on their own lived experience with an eye to its relevance to the project and the site. Their own prior experience was a critical factor in the ways each shaped her role, interacted with various participants, and interpreted the contexts of the centers and the university. Personal change came against the backdrop of prior experience. This was also true of the participating administrators, teachers, center staff, and NYU team members. Therefore, who facilitators are, what they know and feel, and how their life experience intersects with their new roles are critical factors for the highly personal work in which they will find themselves immersed. Equally important is the identification of those factors in the institutional context and in the reform effort itself that support or detract from the personal and professional change that this new role requires.

Our understanding of the importance of the center director or school principal in the change process was reaffirmed by this project. As capable as the site facilitators were, they could not effect change alone. Where there was strong, positive leadership, the site facilitator was free to work across the center and was supported in doing so. There, the project was shaped to fit the context and has become an essential aspect of the center's modus operandi. Where leadership was poor, diffuse, or antagonistic, the site facilitators had to continually focus on supporting teachers in their day-to-day efforts to teach in child-centered ways. In these settings, the project took root with individual teachers in individual classrooms. Where it expanded beyond the full-day classrooms that were our original targets, it did so as something of a subversive activity among individual teachers sending definite underground ripples centerwide.

In decisions about who should spearhead change initiatives in schools, it is often asked whether one should choose from outside of or within the organization. Our initial decision was to choose facilitators from outside of the Head Start centers. Now, 4 years later, we are sure that for our project we were correct. The site facilitators asked questions, crossed social boundaries, and inquired about accepted norms in ways that were not possible to insiders or to individuals, such as a new education director in the employ of the center. They worked with site directors in ways unavailable to others in the centers.

Our project was designed to phase out the site facilitators at the end of the 3rd year. The NYU team was to maintain contact and provide support where necessary during the 4th year. It is affirmative testimony to the work of the site facilitators that this time frame was both practicable and successful. In each center, the project has been implemented in ways that reflect the context of the center. Could we have done more had we more time? Definitely. Four years is too short a time for this transformative work. However, we leave knowing that all the centers, even the most resistant, have changed dramatically and, probably, irrevocably in this time.

For our final word, we turn to a topic that Jennifer raises: How long can a site facilitator provide intensive support in an under-resourced setting in which there are generally low expectations for the important work of teaching and learning? This may be the most important question emerging from our project since it has implications for reform initiatives at all levels of schooling. Our experience makes it clear that site facilitators cannot be sent into the work of school reform without a strong support network. They need the time and space, alone and in company with trusted colleagues, to reflect on their own lived experience and to look for the connections between what they know and the goals of the change process itself. Moreover, we suspect that continual opportunities to redefine and reshape their activities as the dynamics of the settings change are also critical factors enabling site facilitators to maintain a high level of involvement. Whether a process as intense as that which we have described here can be sustained over a long period of time is something that might be the focus of further research. Swimming with and against the currents can be exhausting, but sometimes it can be good exercise and exhilarating. It depends on the lifeboats.

REFERENCES

Clandinin, D. J., & Connelly, F. M. (1995). *Teachers' professional knowledge landscapes*. New York: Teachers College Press.

Cochran-Smith, M. (1995). Uncertain allies: Understanding the boundaries of race and teaching. *Harvard Educational Review, 65*(4), 541–570.

Cochran-Smith, M., & Lytle, S. (Eds.). (1993). *Inside/Outside: Teacher research and knowledge*. New York: Teachers College Press.

Ely, M., Miller, L. P., Rust, F. O'C., & Krasnow, M. H. (1994, 1995, 1996, 1997, 1998). Unpublished year-end reports on Teaching for Success project to the Robin Hood Foundation. New York: New York University.

Freidus, H. (1996, April). *The co-construction of professional knowledge*. Paper presented at the annual meeting of the American Educational Research Association, New York.

Fullan, M. (1993). *Change forces: Probing the depths of educational reform*. New York: Falmer Press.

Fullan, M. (1997). Emotions and hope: Constructive concepts for complex times. In A. Hargreaves (Ed.), *Rethinking educational change with heart and mind. 1997 ASCD Yearbook* (pp. 216–233). Alexandria, VA: Association for Supervision and Curriculum Development (ASCD).

Fuller, F. (1969). Concerns of teachers: A developmental conceptualization. *American Educational Research Journal, 6*(2), 207–226.

Gardner, H. (1999). *The disciplined mind*. New York: Simon & Schuster.

Garman, N. (1990). Theories embedded in the events of clinical supervision: A hermeneutic approach. *Journal of Curriculum and Supervision, 5*(3), 201–13.

Gitlin, A., & Price, K. (1992). Teacher empowerment and the development of voice. In C. Glickman (Ed.), *Supervision in transition. 1992 ASCD Yearbook* (pp. 61–74). Alexandria, VA: ASCD.

Hall, G. E., Wallace, R. C., & Dorset, W. A. (1973). *A developmental conceptualization of the adopting process within educational institutions*. Austin: University of Texas Research and Development Center for Teacher Education. (ERIC Document Reproduction Service No. ED 095 126)

High/Scope Educational Research Foundation. (1991). *Child observation record*. Ypsilanti, MI: High/Scope Press.

Lieberman, A. (Ed.) (1988). *Building a professional culture in schools*. New York: Teachers College Press.

Lincoln, Y., & Guba, E. (1985). *Naturalistic inquiry.* Beverly Hills, CA: Sage.

Loucks-Horsely, S., & Stiegelbauer, S. (1991). Using knowledge of change to guide staff development. In A. Lieberman & L. Miller (Eds.), *Staff development for education in the '90s* (pp. 15–36). New York: Teachers College Press.

McLaughlin, M. (1993). What matters most in teachers' workplace context? In J. W. Little & M. W. McLaughlin (Eds.), *Teachers' work: Individuals, colleagues, and context* (pp. 79–103). New York: Teachers College Press.

Philliber Research Associates. (1994, 1995, 1996, 1997, 1998). Unpublished reports to the Robin Hood Foundation on COR data. New York: Philliber Research Associates.

Rust, F. O'C. (1989). How supervisors think about teaching. *Journal of Teacher Education, 39*(2), 56–64.

Sarason, S. (1990). *The predictable failure of educational reform.* San Francisco: Jossey-Bass.

Chapter 2

From Ideal to Real: Unlocking the Doors of School Reform

Cynthia McCallister

Ellen, a reading teacher, approaches a classroom where she has been working regularly with the teacher and students as they implement a literacy instruction program that involves various forms of group instruction, continuous monitoring of student progress, and push-in supplemental instruction that requires collaborative planning among teachers. Ellen has sensed growing resistance, even hostility from the teacher. Today when she comes to the classroom, she finds the door locked. She knocks, and the teacher unlocks the door to let Ellen inside. Some days later Ellen and I reflect on the teacher's new habit of locking the door from the inside and agree the gesture is meaningful. A door locked from the inside is a metaphor for the challenges we've faced as we implement a schoolwide literacy program. We agree that mere humans can't move through locked doors and consider the conditions that need to exist in order to keep them open.

As a person who inadvertently found herself working in the unfamiliar terrain of school reform, I reflect here on my experiences as a staff developer and parent in order to understand the forces that lock doors from within, preventing change in the core practices of schooling. Writing from the perspective of a participant in a school reform initiative, and not from that of a scholar of school reform, I will attempt to explain the challenges I faced in my work and to offer personal insights that were borne of my experience. While some of the insights I present might challenge emerging tenets found in the school reform literature, they nevertheless offer a perspective that is grounded in a particular social context.

INSCRIBING THE IDEAL

On a sweltering afternoon in late August of 1996, I became involved in the life of a school that I'll refer to here as the Friendship School. I had recently relocated to New York City to begin my new position as assistant professor of literacy education at a nearby university, and I had been trying to locate a public school with a progressive orientation for my children, then 5 and 6. With children in tow, I wandered into the Friendship School, a public primary-intermediate school in northern Manhattan. There I met the principal and spent time exploring, admiring classrooms, and chatting with members of the faculty who were readying their classrooms in the days prior to the opening of school. Before I left, I applied to enroll my children, and when I returned home later that evening, I received word that they would be accepted.

This school would open its doors to students for the first time in the fall of 1996, originating from parents' struggle for a learner-centered school of choice in the community school district. It is located in a highly diverse, economically depressed community in New York City and is supported by a private foundation that promotes systemic school reform by funding innovative educational plans. The organizers of the school recruited and hired teachers who were committed to implementing an innovative curriculum based on progressive, student-centered pedagogy; involving parents in the educational experiences of students; and promoting social justice for culturally, socially, and linguistically diverse students. The school comprises three small programs: a dual-language primary elementary program, a regular primary elementary program, and a middle school program. The dual-language primary program and the middle school program were the ones I was involved in and report on in this study. Within this population, 85 percent of the students were Latino; 80 percent were eligible for the free lunch program.

Not long after the school year began, I met with the principal and several teachers to outline plans for an ongoing professional development project designed to strengthen literacy programs. I volunteered to work with the teachers on a bimonthly basis, and as a result a teacher inquiry group was formed. Inquiry groups have become a popular approach to professional development and critical reflection for teachers (Graves, 1983). Typically, the focus of inquiry groups is to examine teaching and learning at the classroom level, but the story of our inquiry group extends beyond the boundaries of classroom walls. The group formed during a time of rapid growth and change, just after the school had opened and when the faculty were beginning to form a collective identity and a vision for what the school would become. The inquiry group was comprised of teachers from kindergarten through fifth grade who met periodically throughout the 1996–1997 school year. The objective of the group was simply to provide a structure for learning and reflection centering on notions of "best practice" in literacy education. Our group meetings usually included a brief presentation on and discussion of topics of relevance to the teachers. The group meetings allowed us to become acquainted, to articulate a common philosophy about literacy education, and to establish goals for the literacy program.

Meetings were held after school and attendance was limited to a small number of regular participants. Often meetings had to be canceled or rescheduled to allow time for more urgent concerns to be addressed. On an individual basis, each teacher was experiencing the intensity of a first year in a new school community. They wanted help and support as they embarked on new ways of teaching, but I was only available to attend the inquiry group meetings after school. Neither the teachers nor I anticipated that the projects and products borne of our inquiry group meetings—objectives for the inquiry group and literacy learning objectives for students—would serve as the foundation for schoolwide program development. But as it evolved, the work of the inquiry group informed and influenced program development for the school as a whole. This had not been our intent, which was to be an informal group attending to the exclusive needs of group members.

From the inquiry group's inception, the principal was interested in and supportive of our work and attended several meetings. She encouraged the group to articulate a literacy program plan that could serve as a blueprint, and suggested the plan might be helpful and relevant for teachers throughout the school. I sketched an outline based on reading and writing workshops (see Figure 2.1), which I was asked to present to the larger faculty during a professional development retreat. I offered a brief overview of a literacy program based on the workshop model (Graves, 1983). I showed a videotape on guided reading (Tabersky, 1996), and I presented an overview of the *New Performance Standards* in *English Language Arts* (New York City Board of Education, 1997). I explained how the workshop model would allow a programmatic context for teachers to address the demands set forth in the standards. There was generally high interest in the program plan. Teachers wanted to know more about the workshop model and about implementation,

FIGURE 2.1. Literacy Program Plan

Objective: Organize classroom structures that...
- Emphasize student engagement, independence, and achievement
- Allow teacher to make observations and assessment, and provide one-on-one, small-group, and whole-class instruction

Daily reading
- Whole-class minilessons (10 minutes)— *Instruction on content, skills, or procedures*
- Independent reading (30-40 minutes) — *Students read independently while teacher conferences with individual students, coordinates literature circles or guided reading groups*
- Whole-group share (10 minutes)
- Read aloud (20-30 minutes)

Daily writing
- Whole-class minilessons (10 minutes)— *Instruction on content, skills, or procedures*
- Independent writing (30-40 minutes)— *Teacher conferences with students in small groups or one-on-one*
- Whole-group share (10 minutes) — for example, "Author's Chair"

Performances and products based on new performance standards
- Annotated lists of books read (general or specific related to genre, author, or theme)
- Reading logs
- Literature circle role sheets
- Audio or video taped read aloud or reader's theater productions
- Literature response papers
- Informative reports
- Oral presentations
- Book reviews
- Autobiographical narratives

management, and assessment of the model. In order to meet their needs, the principal arranged a 2-hour staff development workshop at which time the teachers viewed a series of four videotapes featuring descriptions of reading conferences and shared, independent, and guided reading approaches (Tabersky, 1996). After the staff viewed the tapes, I circulated a questionnaire asking for the teachers' responses to the instructional approaches presented. These responses provided a baseline assessment of teachers' needs, interests, and concerns. (A summary of these responses appears in Figure 2.2.)

After it was apparent that there was unified support for adopting a literacy program based on reading and writing workshop models, the next step was to articulate these principles into a formal program that could serve as a functional document to guide the organization, management, and assessment of literacy programs. I took responsibility for developing a more complete literacy program document that could be used by teachers in grades K–8, and then circulated the program document to the faculty for feedback. A committee comprised of parents and faculty met to discuss the plan and provided feedback and commentary, which I incorporated into a final draft. The result was a cohesive, K–8 literacy program that was accepted by all teachers. The literacy program aligns with the new standards for language education issued jointly by the International Reading Association and the National Council of Teachers of English (1996). The plan was submitted and subsequently approved by the district administration. This document was also incorporated into a grant proposal that a committee comprised of parents and members of the faculty were planning to submit to a private foundation that provided funding support for educational innovations in New York City. The grant proposal explicitly stated that the language and literacy instruction in the school would follow guidelines specified in the literacy plan. Our school subsequently received a 5-year commitment of funding from the private reform organization.

MAKING THE IDEAL INTO THE REAL

The faculty, the principal, and I arrived at the decision that any substantive change would come only with sustained, institutionally supported staff development. The foundation grant provided funding to assist in the implementation of our reform programs. The principal dedicated a portion of the grant to fund my position as staff developer.

When our school opened for its 2nd year in the fall of 1997, my status changed from parent-volunteer to staff developer. I was hired for

FIGURE 2.2. Teacher Responses to Reading Workshop Approaches

What aspects of your program need the most immediate attention in order to implement the new literacy curriculum?
- Managing and organizing the classroom
- Helping students become independent readers and writers
- Implementing activities and expectations that emphasize student independence (freeing the teacher to work independently with students)
- Organizing instruction that focuses on students' needs

What obstacles do you see in terms of making changes and/or implementing literacy workshops in your classroom?
- The need for "another pair of hands"
- Fostering student engagement
- Meeting the developmental needs of emergent readers and middle school students
- Addressing the needs of "high maintenance" students
- Obtaining necessary materials
- Meeting the demands of second-language learners who have limited English proficiency
- Space limitations
- Wide range of abilities of students in the classroom

What supports do you believe you need in order to make needed changes in your literacy program?
- Materials, training, and someone to visit and assist me in the classroom
- More books on a variety of different levels
- Weekly sharings of students' work in team meetings that model sharings done in literacy workshop
- A united schoolwide plan or strategy that really works (even though individual styles may vary)
- Regular meetings on the progress of literacy program concerns, and sharing things that work
- Management and organizational models
- Staff development, class intervisitation, and school intervisitation

What elements would you like to see written into the New Visions implementation plan in terms of providing support for your literacy program?
- More outreach from universities in our rooms so that we can implement programs based on faculty research
- Development of study groups within the school to discuss literacy and books we are reading
- Teacher time for a study group

a yearlong period to assist in the implementation of the newly adopted literacy program. I used insights generated by the questionnaire (see Figure 2.2) to inform my work as a staff developer. Based on my assessment of faculty needs, I outlined a strategy of professional development that included the following components:

- Biweekly study group meetings
- Classroom-based consultation and demonstrations by consultants
- Monthly staff development workshops
- Biannual literacy colloquium (outside consultants invited to provide staff development)
- Classroom-based consultation and demonstrations by teacher-director, early childhood specialist, and literacy consultant

When the plan had been introduced in the spring of 1997, all teachers had expressed a strong commitment to the program. However, the plan lost the support of many teachers when it came time to undertake the work of implementation. Throughout the fall of 1997, I visited classrooms and consulted with teachers and administrators to address the challenges of implementation. Though several teachers demonstrated a firm commitment to the program, read widely, and searched me out in order to discuss implementation problems and predicaments, many teachers either ignored the program or gradually developed resistance to me and the reading teachers who were responsible for assisting in the implementation.

One of the three programs within the school refused to participate in program implementation. In the remaining two programs—those that became the focus of my involvement—approximately half the teachers made an earnest effort to adopt program structures. While some teachers demonstrated their enthusiasm by participating with curiosity and a willingness to engage in critical reflection, others merely went through the superficial motions of changing time and grouping structures. When they were urged to engage in assessment and instruction approaches that were embedded in the literacy workshop structures, many began to resist the program. In a metaphorical sense, doors began to lock from the inside.

At the same time that we were attempting to implement our new schoolwide literacy program, a citywide after-school supplemental reading program was introduced. Most of the classroom teachers who had regularly attended our inquiry group meetings were now assigned after-school instructional groups. The district initiative interfered with the previously planned monthly staff development workshops, and due to scheduling conflicts, these sessions could not be rescheduled. Additionally, a variety of unforeseen problems, such as the need for staff coverage when teachers were absent and administrative tasks that pulled reading teachers from their intended work with students in classrooms, resulted in lost support for classroom teachers trying to implement the new program. In the face of huge professional demands, teachers lost interest in the after-school inquiry group, and after the winter break, the season of test preparation and the anxiety it produced put a stranglehold on our best intentions to bring about our ideal.

By February our literacy program was in a beleaguered state. I noticed that in many classrooms students were reading and writing during workshop time; but teacher-student interactions that served as a context for assessment and instruction were minimal. Little progress had been made in terms of building teaching capacity around the aims of the literacy program. Meanwhile, the superintendent's support for the interim acting principal waned, as did needed resources and necessary freedom from bureaucratic mandates that sabotaged the intent of the reform. Faculty and parents who wanted the interim acting principal to be appointed to a permanent position became involved in struggle with the superintendent who wanted her replaced. Over the course of the 1st and 2nd years, faculty morale deteriorated, and most of the original faculty eventually left the school.

Given the unstable political context surrounding the school, the relative level of inexperience among the teachers, and the lack of policy and administrative support structures to sustain teachers during innovation, I began to believe that the work of building schoolwide instructional programs that stem from student assessment had probably been an unrealistic expectation. However, though the progress was less than I'd hoped for, I wanted to better understand what had gone wrong. As I began to conceptualize a plan for the formative evaluation phase of this project, my inquiry was directed around the double question of how the various participants understood the specific challenges of program implementation and how they addressed them. I had three objectives:

- To identify and make sense of the challenges encountered in program implementation from the teachers' perspectives
- To identify real and potential strategies and solutions articulated by teachers to overcome challenges
- To offer strategies for moving toward student-centered curriculum that might work, given the characteristics of this school context

Midway through the 2nd year, I circulated a survey to assess teachers' perceptions of the challenges of program implementation and the supports in place (or needed) to assist in the process. Reinforcing my sense that many of the teachers were becoming cynical about the program and disinterested in pursuing further involvement, fewer than 30 percent returned the questionnaire. Thus, the data generated offer an incomplete picture of the needs of the faculty. Nonetheless, the data do present an understanding of some of the challenges we faced and the supports that were in place. Further, I think that the insights of those who responded provide a picture of how the program worked in those places where it had been implemented.

As I read the survey responses, it was immediately clear that there were conspicuous silences in the feedback I had gotten. I suspected the silences meant something. I was aware the program had been a source of tension in the school, and I wanted to understand the sources of conflict as a means to understanding the process of how our school underwent change.

COMBING THE NOISE

My work in this school reform account reminds me of the adage, "a fish is the last to find water." The depth of my involvement as an invested participant in the school interfered with my ability to objectively assess the circumstances of implementation. Some teachers resisted my involvement and support, while others welcomed me and invited my participation in their classrooms. The latter were the teachers with whom I shared a sense of purpose and intent and who seemed to understand the aims of the program. My involvement with these individuals provided a reality context against which I interpreted our progress toward the goals we articulated in the literacy plan. To achieve an understanding of our progress in implementing the literacy plan from a multitude of perspectives, I conducted in-depth interviews with those teachers with whom I worked most closely. These were the three reading teachers and several classroom teachers who were involved in implementing the new literacy program. I analyzed and interpreted the data from the interviews in order to build an understanding of the forces that influenced the progress of our reform.

Cohesion and Climate

One of the central goals of the literacy program was to establish a climate of inquiry in each classroom where learning expectations were consistent for students from classroom to classroom and grade level to grade level. In classrooms where the program was "working," an observer might find students reading books or participating in literature discussion groups while the teacher circulated among students, assessing and teaching. The challenge of creating these types of environments came out in interviews with reading teachers. When the program worked, the benefits were obvious. One reading teacher commented:

> In Nan's class, you walk in and you know. There are charts on the walls, evidence of reading instruction, and a plan. There is differential instruction in whole, small, and individual groups. There is evidence of student assessment via conferencing—the teacher one-to-one with the child. The teacher is reading and taking notes. The observations are kept in a folder. We take notes and paste them into a binder. I know where they're coming from. It's smooth. I blend in; the kids know the routines. It's an easy flow.

In classrooms where the program was not being followed according to the established plan, the learning environment had a different feeling. As one reading teacher commented:

> I don't see a concrete program going on. I would like to know what these teachers are doing in terms of literacy, how they're doing it, so that I can understand the kids and work with them more effectively. For the teachers who are not following the program, it's a lot of guessing and wondering. I don't see whole-class instruction or small-group instruction. No evidence of any kind of program. There I have to develop my own program and relationships. It's like I'm the teacher and I'm developing the program on my own. The disadvantage is it takes longer, and there aren't as many signs of success, not one road to success—less clear to the kids themselves.

In these classrooms, teachers frequently changed their classroom schedules without notice, thus forcing reading teachers to pull children out of the class while they were involved in some subject other than reading (choice time, for example). This left reading teachers feeling conflicted and anxious about students who might have been missing important learning experiences.

Commitment

When teachers saw evidence of learning, commitment to strategies that seemed to be working were intensified. One teacher articulated her commitment to the program in this way:

Well, I think it is very challenging. It is tiring, I go home and I'm really tired. A lot of times I work late into the night. It is frustrating sometimes. But I feel like there is so much more to do and much more to learn, but it makes me feel like I'm learning, like I'm stretching myself. I'm really growing. It gives me the energy to keep going, to pursue it. I feel very passionate about it. It's not only exciting but it makes sense to teach this way, for everyone. The children are excited, we are excited.

This level of commitment to professional development centered on the literacy program was rare in the school.

As the year progressed, it became clear to me that the supports necessary for program success were missing. For example, inexperienced teachers had difficulty balancing the multiple, simultaneous demands of assessing students, analyzing and interpreting assessment data, and planning instruction. Many teachers in the school who were new to the profession of teaching were preoccupied with the demands of classroom management. In most cases there was limited alignment between the program ideals and what occurred in practice. Only a few teachers were committed to using the workshop structure as a context for curriculum-embedded assessment and instruction, a critical feature of the literacy program plan. Also, as teachers "locked doors" in the figurative sense and stopped working with the staff members who had greater expertise, programs were changed and modified to the point that they resembled traditional core practices.

EXPECTATIONS AND ACCOUNTABILITY

The expectation of program accountability seemed to be generally lacking in the school. From the beginning, teachers seemed unevenly committed to the program. The principal explained to the faculty at a meeting in the beginning of the year that the literacy plan was submitted to the district office as a substitute for the commercial program and on that basis it was to be followed. However, because incentive structures to support this expectation were not in place, teachers seemed to feel free to create their own programs without challenge or encouragement to work collaboratively within the adopted model. When conflict arose out of teachers' resistance to the program, their resistance went unchallenged for lack of incentives to motivate them to move through the conflict.

Perhaps part of the administration's reluctance in setting firm expectations had to do with its commitment to teacher autonomy. Many of the teachers had been attracted to the school because it offered the opportunity to exercise greater freedom in interpreting curriculum and using personal, professional judgment. The school had developed around an ethos of deep respect for teachers' expertise. Teachers were viewed by the administration as skilled professionals whose prerogative it was to interpret curriculum and set up classroom structures. Thus, while many teachers were hired because of their commitment to progressive, student-centered practices (maybe even because of this perception of teachers' commitment), there were few expectations that teachers' work with their students would be scrutinized with respect to their students' achievement.

Conflict

In my work with teachers in the school, I observed that growth and change inevitably brought forth some sort of dissonance, either internal or external. Internal dissonance occurred when a teacher recognized that something wasn't working or needed to be changed and assumed responsibility for carrying out the necessary changes. In these cases, dissonance was generative in the sense of the teacher's intentions aligning with the intentions of the program or the norms of the community. But external dissonance—between individuals—was brought about when individuals resisted change or reconciliation of differences because they either didn't understand the changes that needed to be made or didn't believe in the intentions and practices of the program or the norms of the community. Unresolved dissonance occurred in the form of hostility or resentment among people involved in change.

When external dissonance went unresolved, it became a destructive force that threatened what one teacher referred to as the "moral fiber" of the community. In many instances, when individuals weren't feeling successful in meeting the demands of program change, they commonly assigned blame to sources other than themselves. Teachers who fell into the latter category complained about the rigidity of the program, reasoned that program demands were impossible due to the lack of student competency or student behavior, claimed they lacked resources (aides or student teachers) to support individual work with students, and that the lack of resources limited their ability to fully implement the program. When this dissonance went unresolved, and teachers were not helped to find strategies to overcome the challenges, they resorted to familiar practices.

One of the reading teachers pointed out that it was necessary for the administration to acknowledge conflict as a natural element of the change process. She commented:

> In a staff meeting, we talked about a rubric, like that process we went through with a teacher who shared student work. That was helpful, but not everyone would be able to do it. The middle school director showed us a tape, and everyone was resistant. She never said, "I want to do this and I understand it's painful and hard because it's the last line of privacy." Once you give them the reason that it's hard, they understand and are more willing to meet the challenge.

Our experiences demonstrate the slow progress of institutional change. Substantive change began in pockets where individual teachers took risks to transform classroom practices, but systemwide change failed to take hold because of teacher inexperience, a lack of institutional expectations and accountability structures that would encourage teachers to follow the literacy program, a lack strategies to help teachers overcome the underlying sources of resistance, and political conflict among the district administration, the school administration, and parent groups.

Teaching as Learning

Teachers were the critical link for program success. The model of instruction called for in the program plan involved teachers in a continual process of learning about students through assessments and then utilizing this source of knowledge to inform instructional decisions. However, for a largely inexperienced teaching staff like ours where six of thirteen classroom teachers were in their 1st year of teaching and three had less than 5 years of experience, this was a tremendous struggle. Classroom management was the order of the day for them, as it is for many beginning teachers. We did not have an adequate structure for teacher learning. We had a few experienced teachers in the school, but their expertise was unavailable as a source of support for these inexperienced teachers. We had not thought to provide assistance for grappling with the challenges of the program. Consequently, there was often limited alignment between the program ideals and actual practice.

In school districts that adopt materials-driven curricula—where, for example, a commercial program is purchased and the administration trusts that students will progress academically if the teachers are trained to use the materials—teaching practice will not change appreciably. In these cases, money is spent on published programs, and teachers are expected to be experts at applying techniques of behavioral engineering (Sadker, 1991). Widely employed models of professional development and curriculum implementation provide approaches to staff development in which school administrators attend district-level meetings and training sessions and then return back to their school buildings where they then supervise the process of translating district-level policy to classroom teachers. This top-down model of staff development isn't equipped to ensure that teachers' voices and their wealth of expertise inform program development, or that the staff development system ultimately builds teacher expertise.

Our literacy program was intended to be student-driven in that it required that teachers monitor student progress and tailor instruction around student needs. This type of program relies on teachers' knowledge about students and their learning, rather than on technical expertise concerning the use of materials. The program we aspired to implement relied upon administrative structures at all levels that nurtured and supported teachers' professional growth, but these structures were nonexistent.

In our story it was the experienced teachers who committed themselves enthusiastically to new learning and change in practice. The more experienced faculty might have been a valuable resource to the inexperienced teachers, but without an explicit staff development system in place, their expertise went untapped.

HARMONIZING THE IDEAL AND THE REAL: STRATEGIES TO SUPPORT PROGRAM IMPLEMENTATION

This school reform story expresses the dissonance that occurs when the tidy and soundless ideals of formal texts such as mission statements and curriculum plans are imported into the boisterous, noisy reality of classrooms and schools where competing interests vie for support and resources. In our instance, policy was written by participants of the school community to serve as a kind of social contract offered to the school's constituents: It informed parents about what their children would be provided; it informed the district of the instructional approaches that would replace the published curriculum used in other districtwide schools; and it provided the faculty with a common set of objectives to guide practice. As I worked in the school, I observed the uneven patterns of program implementation and began to wonder and worry about the forces that inhibited success. The challenge I faced was to understand the patterns of the noisy dissonance and to explore ways in which often-conflicting efforts could be harmonized. The lessons I learned converge around several themes, each of which I will discuss in turn.

Ensure Close Fidelity to Program Specifications

Schools sometimes undertake reforms that require teachers to operate within conceptual and practical frames that are out of the range of individual or institutional competence (Elmore, 1996; Fullan, 1993; Fullan with Stielgelbauer, 1991). As a result the reforms are sometimes trivialized versions of new ideas, and structures are only superficially modified and ultimately fail to change the core practices of teaching and learning (Elmore, 1996). In the situation described here, the tension between accountability to the program and professional autonomy was a great concern. As I've pointed out, teachers in our school were hired because of their commitment to progressive, student-centered practices. Many were attracted to the school because it offered the opportunity to exercise greater freedom in interpreting curriculum and using personal, professional judgment and to approach teaching in a nontraditional manner. Ironically, this was probably the greatest source of tension since the program required a commitment on the part of individual teachers to suspend personally favored approaches in order to try out approaches that were specified in the literacy plan. The tension between faculty autonomy and accountability to the adopted program needed to have been addressed if the program were to have succeeded. The complexities of the organization, including the need for more collaboration among faculty; conflict between various levels of the administration; lack of district support for the school leadership; and friction between members of the faculty—all inhibited a reconciliation between faculty accountability to program expectations and teachers' need for professional autonomy.

Develop Learning Structures

Thompson and Zeuli (1999) stress that an institution's capacity to sustain reform hinges upon its ability to promote learning: "The point here is not to replicate specific programs but to widen the circles of people who understand how to design and conduct programs appropriate to their own settings" (p. 44). The literacy program was conceived within a small circle of learning, and plans for bringing the program to scale within the school called for strategies to widen the circles of learning. Though participants attempted to create new circles and widen existing ones, these efforts were repeatedly scattered by political and institutional winds. The instability caused by faculty turnover was the greatest threat to the literacy program. Without the continued commitment of a critical mass of teachers and without the leadership of a principal who supported the program, the outcomes of our early program implementation efforts evaporated.

Resolve the Paradox of Progressive Educational Practice

In progressive education there are implicit as well as formal standards. Implicit standards call for teachers to follow leads and the needs of students as they collaboratively construct curriculum with them. The challenge for progressive educators is to balance student-centered practices with community norms and expectations. More time is needed for staff development intended to assist teachers in working through this paradox. But teachers need to be supported through this process with the guidance of exemplary teachers who understand progressive approaches that meet the demands of educational standards. Continued staff development is required by school systems seeking to change existing instructional practices in order to assist the teachers in developing curriculum and teaching approaches that allow them to simultaneously acknowledge both sets of standards.

Utilize Mentorship and Staff Development

One major accomplishment of the implementation of the literacy program was the mentoring and development of experienced teachers who became "experts" on the most innovative and technologically advanced methods of literacy instruction. But, as Elmore (1996) points out, "the existence of exemplars, without some way of capitalizing on their talents, only reinforces the notion that ambitious teaching is an individual trait, not a professional expectation" (p. 15). Teachers like these are important resources for a faculty. Any long-term plan for continued growth and change should utilize their expertise in a well-planned system of mentoring and staff development. In order for substantial change to occur, teachers need the support of inside expertise.

Gordon, Bonilla-Bowman, Cohen, and Lemons (1993) suggest that substantive changes in the core practices of schooling might require a revision of the administrative structures designed to support staff development. Their insights about the Performance Assessment Collaboratives for Education (PACE) might well be applied to the literacy program implementation at our school:

> To do this kind of teaching well may require more direction, demonstration, structure and supervision than is traditional in the decentralized management approach to educational administration. Once newly acquired strengths are in place, teachers may be ready for greater autonomy in further development and change of the conceptual model. (p.55)

Provide Systemwide Administrative Support Structures

The change initiative presented here took place in a district whose administrative systems discouraged innovation and school autonomy. The school faced resistance in its efforts to reform educational practice in a variety of ways. For example, each school in the district is mandated to follow a commercially published instructional basal reading program. When our school submitted an alternative to the basal plan, the district reluctantly approved the plan. However, our school received 75 percent less funding for books than that provided other schools in the district. In a literature-based reading program, books are the basis of the language arts curriculum, and scarce resources seriously disadvantage students' opportunities to learn.

The politics of leadership also inhibited program success. In spite of the parents' collective desire to appoint the interim acting principal to a permanent position, the superintendent explained publicly that he did not support her appointment. For 2 years the school operated without a permanently appointed principal while the parents' association and the superintendent waged a war over school leadership. The principal was forced to operate with inadequate support. For 1½ years the school went without an assistant principal entirely. An assistant principal was finally appointed in the spring of 1998 by the superintendent, who disregarded the teachers' and parents' wishes and appointed an administrator from the district office.

CONCLUSION

"Local invention," writes Darling-Hammond (1997), "must be supported by policies that provide a mix of top-down support and bottom-up initiatives" (p. 337). This is the crux of the dilemma that I have attempted to portray in this chapter. I have struggled to write a conclusion to this story that ties up all the loose ends by way of an insightful explanation. Since I have been intimately involved in this story in multiple roles—as a parent, a researcher, and a staff developer—the task of summing up the larger significance of this experience has been difficult inasmuch as my perspective is shaped by my involvement.

During a recent family camping trip I found myself in a situation that struck me as a fitting metaphor for the story told here. On this trip, we got a late start and reached our camp site well after dark. This was bad planning because the first order of business when you're in the woods is to start a fire, and it's hard to start a fire in the dark. Dew settles after sundown, making the wood damp and resistant to heat. Tools are hard to find in the darkness. Time and energy are spent searching for matches, kindling, and wood. Anxiety and frustration take hold. On this particular night, we eventually got our fire started, and the warmth of the blaze created the campfire ambiance that lures us time and again into the woods for family camping trips.

Professional development is like making a campfire. Our initiative started as a flame. The program described above began as an idea among a small group of optimistic, like-minded members of a tightly knit school community. We spent time at first fumbling in the damp darkness, but we were motivated with hope and commitment. Eventually our flame caught and seemed to grow stronger for a time. But the flame of reform was extinguished, again and again, by the rain and winds of an institutional system that was not supportive of our efforts. Numerous contextual complexities interfered with the smooth and successful implementation of the program.

At the time of this writing—over 2 years after I first began my work as a staff developer—the landscape of the school has changed beyond recognition. After a long and bitter fight that eventually divided parents, the principal was not appointed. When the principal was not appointed, the middle school director and many teachers left the school to take positions elsewhere. Shortly thereafter the superintendent took a position in another city. From the original group of a dozen or so teachers with whom I worked, only one teacher remains at the school. The school has seen three principals in 5 years, and the current principal has been unsuccessful in garnering support from fractious subgroups of the school community. As new teachers and administrators have come to fill the shoes of their predecessors, a new culture has evolved with markedly different aims and intentions than those that characterized the culture of the founding members of the school.

In most schools and classrooms, core practices don't change on a large scale because reform efforts don't sufficiently account for the complexity of how institutions are organized and what incentive structures govern practice (Darling-Hammond, 1997; Elmore, 1996). Schools typically aren't organized to harness the power of individuals or to promote interpersonal learning among colleagues. Unless organizational structures are changed to promote collegial learning, reforms are likely to fail. This was a problem we hadn't sufficiently anticipated as we planned our staff development program. The success of our literacy program hinged on the capacity of our school to build a self-sustaining learning community and on the capacity of that community to maintain the momentum for change. The program relied on individual teachers whose enthusiasm, interest, and expertise could be harnessed to guide collective professional learning. The flame of reform in our school was held by these teachers. But the environment did not support their leadership. The program might have succeeded if the environment had been more supportive of their growth and more mindful about ways to encourage their sharing of expertise. With greater stability and more coherent intentions across the layers of the institutional context, their expertise might have been cultivated and might have become a source of energy to keep the fire burning. Instead, every accomplishment seemed to fade, and we were forced to begin again where we had started. Those of us in this story who worked to transform teaching practices found ourselves continually trying to start fires in the dark.

REFERENCES

Darling-Hammond, L. (1997). *The right to learn.* San Francisco: Jossey-Bass.

Elmore, R. (1996). Getting to scale with good educational practice. *Harvard Educational Review, 66*(1), 1–26.

Fullan, M. (1993). *Change forces.* New York: Falmer Press.

Fullan, M. (with Stiegelbauer, S.). (1991). *The new meaning of educational change.* New York: Teachers College Press.

Gordon, E. W., Bonilla-Bowman, C., Cohen, S., & Lemons, M. P. (1993). *Report of the external evaluation of PACE (Portfolio Assessment Collaboratives in Education), Year One 1992–1993.* (Unpublished report funded by the Rockefeller Foundation)

Graves, D. H. (1983). *Writing: Teachers and children at work.* Portsmouth, NH: Heinemann.

New York City Board of Education (1997). _New performance standards in English language arts._

Sadker, M. (1991). _Teachers, schools, and society_ (2nd ed.). New York: McGraw-Hill.

Tabersky, S. (1996). _A close-up look at teaching reading: Focusing on children and our goals_ [video series]. Portsmouth, NH: Heinemann.

Thompson, C. L., & Zeuli, J. S. (1999). The frame and the tapestry: Standards-based reform and professional development. In L. Darling-Hammond & G. Sykes (Eds.), _Teaching as the learning profession_: Handbook of policy & practice (pp. 341–375). San Francisco: Jossey-Bass.

Chapter 3

Implementing Curriculum Change: Lessons from the Field

Helen Freidus, Claudia Grose, and Margaret McNamara

In recent years there has been a call for research that examines the process of school change through a wider lens. Linda Darling-Hammond (1998) has cited the need for studies of the ways in which teachers make transitions from the more passive model of transmission-oriented teaching to a transactional model in which teaching supports the active engagement of all children. To this end, she poses two important questions for consideration:

1. What kinds of professional development really make a difference in helping teachers to think and act in new ways?
2. In what ways does the particular context of a school or community facilitate and/or constrain this process?

A similar need has been voiced by scholars focusing on specific curriculum change. Dick Allington (1997) has cautioned that much of current research on literacy is being conducted in a "too small box." How, he asks, can we broaden our perspectives to gain an understanding of literacy instruction within a larger context? If we believe that reading, writing, and language development shape and are shaped by the world of the learner, then our research should reflect a more holistic perspective.

Working with related concerns, Penelope Peterson (1998) has raised a set of questions regarding validity in educational research. Motivated by her son's questions about how her work on educational reform would make a difference in his school, she takes seriously his challenge: "What good are you doing anyway?" (p. 4). Why, she wonders, have the contributions of research remained so limited in their influence on teachers and policy makers. If the findings of research are only considered significant by other researchers, how valid can they be? How can we create closer connections between the work of research, professional development, and instruction?

This chapter has been shaped as a response to these issues and concerns. We look at our work as researchers documenting the implementation of an innovative literacy curriculum in four urban public schools as an opportunity to tell a story of school change. It is a story in which school culture, teacher beliefs, professional development processes, administrative decisions, and school structures all have an impact upon teachers' instructional practices and students' outcomes.

We came to the study as both researchers and teacher educators with a belief that learning is a socially constructed process, influenced by the culture and needs of both learners and teachers (Moll, 1999; Vygotsky, 1922–35/1978). To this, we have added a belief that our own learning and the learning of the educators with whom we worked is and was situated within a particular physical and social context (Hargreaves, 1996; Putnam & Borko, 2000). We see knowledge as shifting and collective. Whatever the role we play, we hold only one piece of the understanding that is necessary to make our work relevant and meaningful.

We see these perspectives as fundamentally related to the literature on school change (Lieberman, 1988; Loucks-Horsely & Stiegelbauer, 1991). These studies show that reform success is contingent not only upon the sincere commitment of teachers and administrators, but also upon the knowledge and skills they bring, their willingness to learn and implement new practices, and the opportunities available to explore and extend what they know and need to know (Fullan, 1993; Hargreaves, 1996; McLaughlin, 1991). Simply put, effective school change requires a recognition of individuals' strengths as well as support for carefully planned experiences that enable insiders and outsiders to develop their ability to join forces and work as a team (Clandinin & Connelly, 1995; Cochran-Smith & Lytle, 1993; Moll, 1999). We have found these conditions hold true not only for teachers and administrators but also for the professional developers who serve in the front lines of the change process.

BACKGROUND

The findings discussed in this chapter emerged from data collected during the academic years 1996–98. These were the first full years of the implementation of *First Steps*, an innovative literacy resource system, in the urban New England public school district in which our research was situated. The study, funded by the Office of Educational Research and Implementation (OERI), was a 3-year collaboration between Bank Street College, the school district, and a major publishing company.

First Steps was developed by the Education Department of Western Australia in 1989. It has been implemented in a broad range of settings in the United States since 1995. Providing a developmentally sequenced approach to instruction, *First Steps* starts from the premise that reading, writing, language, and spelling are integrated components of literacy education. It defines itself not as a literacy program but as a systematic organization of "best practices" that link assessment and instruction. Rather than providing a kit or specific readers and workbooks of its own, *First Steps* is designed to support and extend a wide range of literacy materials and curricular practices.

The goal of *First Steps* is to give teachers (1) effective ways of identifying children's strengths and needs through observation, (2) efficient ways of recording their observations, and (3) explicit strategies for teaching to and extending those identified strengths. It is expected that teachers will need and receive ongoing support and professional development in order to be successful. The support is most frequently provided through a "teacher of teachers" model of professional development. To this end, district personnel are trained by *First Steps* personnel to assist their colleagues in the implementation process.

This chapter explores the complexities of this teacher of teachers model, looking carefully at the ways in which it intersects with the prior knowledge, beliefs, and expectations of both the teachers and professional developers engaged in the process. We describe the professional development model of *First Steps* and analyze the ways in which it has been implemented in the context of our setting. We look at the actual roles played by the professional developers (Tutors), examining the ways in which their identified and hidden needs and concerns affected their ability to execute their role during the initial phase of implementation. In an effort to better understand this dynamic, we then examine the ways in which school and district organizational and support structures affected the Tutors' roles and, ultimately, their efficacy. Finally, we look at the strengths and potential pitfalls involved in implementing a teacher of teachers professional development model and the implications for its widespread use.

THE *FIRST STEPS* PROFESSIONAL DEVELOPMENT MODEL

First Steps takes the position that literacy instruction is most effective when participating schools understand and buy into not only its practices but also its belief system. There is a request that a whole school makes a commitment to the model before embarking on training and implementation. Accordingly, an overview is provided to interested schools or districts before they make their decisions. *First Steps* consultants, usually former teachers or administrators from Western Australia who have used *First Steps* in their classrooms, provide an introduction to the philosophy and practice that underlies the four literacy elements. They also use these meetings to share the beliefs on which *First Steps* is based. These are as follows:

- Teachers view the development of reading, writing, and language arts as integrated processes and, in systematic ways, structure their instruction accordingly.
- Teachers routinely engage in both long- and short-term curriculum planning and design.
- Teachers routinely allocate opportunities for students to read and write on a regular, sustained basis.

Although *First Steps* views all four literacy components as interrelated, for training and early mastery purposes, each element is introduced separately. The expectation is that implementation and mastery of theory and pedagogy will develop over time. Following the introductory sessions, decisions are made at the school or district level about the area that is to be first targeted. It will be several months to a year or two before the next component is undertaken.

Once the school makes a commitment to *First Steps*, professional development in the form of a 2-day introductory course in the targeted area is offered to all teachers. In our study it was writing that was initially chosen. Teachers in the first schools making a commitment to implementation had *First Steps* consultants as instructors. Subsequently, Tutors—veteran teachers who had been selected by their schools or by the district to assume the role of teachers of teachers—led the introductory courses. These Tutors had participated in an 8-day course that provided them with an overview of the four literacy components of *First Steps*. A critical component of this course had been the modeling of professional development methods and materials designed to facilitate the implementation of *First Steps*.

THE STORY OF SOUTHTOWN

In Spring of 1995, Southtown was facing a state education reform effort emerging from increased concern about low scores on standardized tests. While looking for a way to address this concern, the coordinator of reading encountered *First Steps* at the annual International Reading Association conference. She was excited by the possibilities presented by this new resource. Upon her return home, she invited one of her reading resource teachers to join her at an 8-day *First Steps* Tutor training session in a nearby state.

There the two women from Southtown had an opportunity to immerse themselves in learning about the "Developmental Continua" (*First Steps* tools for assessment), examine writing samples, observe videotapes of *First Steps* implementation in Australian classrooms, and discuss strategies for presenting this content to others. As they gained a better understanding of the structures through which *First Steps* helps teachers link assessment and instruction, they came to believe that it could address an aspect of instructional practice that was sorely missing in many of Southtown's classrooms. Enthusiastically they began to consult with *First Steps* personnel about an implementation plan for their own district.

The two women returned to the district and submitted their plan to the superintendent and the language arts coordinator for approval. Southtown, at this time, was facing new state standards regarding student outcomes in writing, standards that the district's educators had not developed resources to address. Consequently, they foresaw that writing could be the district's point of entry into *First Steps*. And so it was.

Initiation

In the autumn of 1995, 31 reading resource teachers, considered to be literacy leaders in Southtown schools, were offered 8 days of professional development in all four components of *First Steps* conducted by *First Steps* personnel. The hope was that the newly trained emissaries would return to their schools, integrate their new resources into their regular work, disseminate information, and generate enthusiasm for the innovation to their colleagues. They would be the catalysts for school-wide commitment to the *First Steps* process.

Just a few months later, in the early months of 1996, all Southtown schools were offered the option of participating in 2-day *First Steps* courses in writing. The courses were fully funded by the district and could be used to fulfill part of the mandated 1996 schoolwide profes-sional development requirement. It was anticipated that the initial re-sponse would be small; the experiences of early volunteers would serve as a pilot model for the rest of the 31 elementary schools in the district.

While this invitation was being extended, the district recruited six teachers who had already participated in the 8-day professional devel-opment experience to serve as Tutors—two would be school based, four would be itinerant. The responsibility of providing training and ongoing support to classroom teachers beginning to implement *First Steps* would be theirs.

To the astonishment of the district, the response to the *First Steps* offering was overwhelming. Southtown teachers and administrators embraced *First Steps* with an enthusiasm that was totally unforeseen. It had been thought that 5–10 schools would be interested in professional development during the first year. Instead, by the fall of 1996, 18 ele-mentary schools requested training, and the numbers kept growing.

The existing district professional development plan had charged the four itinerant Tutors with faculty training and support. Newly trained and barely experienced with *First Steps* pedagogy, these Tutors bore the responsibility for supporting the rapidly expanding implementation. Most Tutors were anxious about their ability to process all the new information they had received. Over and over, the Tutors confided that "It [the Tutor training] was clear at the time, but then when I thought about it later it was overwhelming," and "It was too much too fast." They felt that they were on very shaky ground. However, they remained enthusiastic and committed to the process of *First Steps* implementa-tion.

The Teachers' Experience

With the ongoing support of consultants from *First Steps*, the Tutors worked hard to make the implementation process successful. Con-sciously or unconsciously, they adhered closely to professional develop-ment behaviors that have been cited in the literature as exemplary (Ful-lan, 1993; Hargreaves, 1996; Lieberman & Miller, 1991; McLaughlin, 1991). They endeavored to forge a program that:

- Developed an environment of trust and collegiality
- Acknowledged learning as a process for adults as well as for children
- Included a mixture of specific-skills training and analytic, reflective practices that help teachers develop broader problem-solving strategies
- Provided experiences to support teachers' belief in their own agency
- Helped teachers and administrators integrate the professional development and school innovation into new or existing goals and practices
- Provided explicit instructional strategies for integrating the innovation into the existing skills, understandings, and attitudes of the learners for whom the innovation is being planned

Drawing on their own teaching and learning experiences, the Tutors recognized the importance of building relationships of trust and collaboration throughout the district. They knew intuitively that implementation needed to be viewed as a process, that it would take time to reach their goals. They said:

> If they don't trust you going into the classroom, then it won't happen. You have to work hard to prevent that "ugh" feeling when they see you coming. Trust takes a long time to happen. It doesn't happen overnight.

Tutors offered teachers both specific-skills training and opportunities for identifying and hypothesizing solutions to problems arising during the implementation phase. They encouraged teachers to take risks, to experiment with the process, and to reflect on their experiences in formal and informal settings.

The *First Steps* professional development they offered was broad based but, where needed, sharply focused. Tutors provided instruction in how to observe and assess children's literacy performance, how to record observational data, and how to connect this information to meaningful instructional practices. To facilitate the implementation of *First Steps* pedagogy, they were available to teachers for individual coaching sessions. They modeled lessons within individual classrooms and offered a variety of workshops targeting specific practices ranging from genre studies to creation of materials.

With the support of building administrators, Tutors provided a range of forums designed to foster problem solving within the context of literacy instruction. Many of these occurred through formal structures including grade-level discussions in which individual experiences were shared, after-school study groups in which teachers were paid stipends to explore methods and materials, and faculty meeting discussions in which time was provided for teachers to set goals, share triumphs, and articulate concerns. Other forums, like luncheon meetings, emerged spontaneously in those schools where Tutors and administrators encouraged teachers to work together independently. As one teacher explained:

> We lunch in the room. We talk to each other. We learn together. When I am having difficulty with a child, I ask, "What do you think will help me?" I show the way I do it, and the other teachers will try to help me. We work together. No one is expected to know it all.

Across the schools, teachers reported that they valued these formal and informal opportunities for ongoing learning. They used terms like "validated," "motivated," and "invigorated" to describe their feelings about the district commitment of time and resources allocated to the implementation process. Teachers made it very clear that these professional development experiences created a climate of respect in which participants were made to feel as if they were participants in a professional community.

The role that Tutors might play in individual classrooms was, at first, less enthusiastically received than the forums they facilitated on neutral turf. Teachers were reluctant to invite Tutors into their classrooms. Tutors were not being hypersensitive when they spoke of the need to battle the "ugh" feeling. Teachers tended to respond to offers of assistance with comments like, "You will have to show me sometime." But for a long time, "sometime" never came. Nonetheless, as Tutors persisted, as teachers began to feel more comfortable with the *First Steps* materials, as the district continued to give the message that *First Steps* was there to stay, and as administrators began to require *First Steps* lessons as part of the teacher evaluation process, invitations into classrooms began to come. By the end of the first year, the Tutors began to feel—and in fact to be—more and more welcome in classrooms.

One Tutor, new to the role of professional development, had been quite troubled by the teachers' seeming resistance to her offers of support. With amazement, she described her year-end experience in the following way:

> I cannot believe how much positive feedback I have gotten from the teachers in my schools. Even people whom I never worked

with have been coming up to thank me for being there and helping them. When I said to them, "But I really have not done anything for you," they answered, "Oh, yes, you have. When we listen to our colleagues and hear what you shared with them, we
feel we have been supported by you too."

By the end of the first year of implementation the enthusiasm for
First Steps was enormous. Teachers who had initially participated in
the implementation process rather reluctantly, viewing the district emphasis on writing as an added burden, were talking about the ways in
which *First Steps* helped them help their students. They felt that both
they and their students were making quantum leaps in their understanding of good writing. The teachers were feeling successful, and this success proved to be highly motivating for teachers and students alike.
Teachers increasingly looked for and found meaningful ways to weave
the reading-writing connections into the ongoing work of the classroom. In the words of one teacher:

> I can see my new understanding being transferred to the children.
> They are becoming more aware of what it means to be good writ-
> ers. Before we used *First Steps*, I never heard children discussing
> the parts of a story, analyzing sentences, mentioning the audience
> for whom they were writing. Now it happens all the time.

The Tutors' Perspective

From the Tutors' perspective the overall picture was not quite so rosy.
The Tutors acknowledged and were proud of their accomplishments,
recognizing that they had contributed a meaningful start to a complex
change process. However, they were not at all certain that adequate
supports were in place to ensure that the *First Steps* innovation would
achieve the potential they envisioned.

The Tutors could see the evidence of the new instructional method-
ologies that were being implemented. Children's writing was beginning
to line the walls of many classrooms. The writing documented that
more writing instruction was being provided in these classrooms and
that this instruction was meeting the needs of a broader range of learners. Moreover, conversations in meetings, hallways, and teachers' rooms
indicated that teachers were beginning to talk more comfortably and
more knowledgeably about their own work and that of their children.

The Tutors, however, were looking for broader changes. They saw
little evidence that the existing skills-based curriculum was moving to-

ward becoming a fully integrated literacy curriculum designed to meet the needs of all children. They were not quite certain why this was not happening or what were expeditious ways to move the process forward. As a result, they had a great deal of doubt about the meaningfulness of their work.

Moreover, while the number of invitations to visit rooms was growing, the Tutors were very much aware that not all teachers were making a commitment to the implementation process. On one hand, the Tutors knew that their heavy schedules would not allow them to fulfill any more requests for help than they were now receiving; on the other hand, they felt that it was their responsibility to facilitate schoolwide change. Caught between a rock and a hard place, they were badgered by feelings of frustration and inadequacy. Taking their responsibilities very, very seriously, they did not know what to do.

EXPLORING THE PROCESS

The research process provided a way of exploring the different perspectives held by teachers and Tutors. Discussions held in interviews and focus groups coupled with data from classroom observations of teachers and Tutors at work indicated that a number of factors posed challenges to the implementation process.

Initial Implementation

In an effort to satisfy the unanticipated large demand for *First Steps* by schools and teachers, administrators turned to their newly created body of Tutors. This led to a significant change in the Tutors' roles. The expected outcomes remained constant. However, the time and opportunity afforded to accomplish these outcomes diminished as the number of teachers who were to be served increased.

From the very beginning of their professional development work the four district Tutors were concerned about their efficacy as itinerant professional developers. They felt that they invariably were missing the teachable moments because of scheduling conflicts. Whereas the two school-based Tutors worked only in their own schools, the district Tutors were expected to carry out a host of other leadership and instructional obligations in addition to their *First Steps* work. All felt significantly overextended.

As school requests continued to multiply, the district continued to increase the commitments of their already fully stretched Tutors. The extended numbers cut even further the amount of time and support Tutors could provide for individual classrooms and limited the time they had for their own sorely needed collaborations. This increased the anxiety and frustration of Tutors who were just learning the program and their roles in the implementation of this program:

Tutor 1: This is a new program. No one has gone before us and set it up. No one can tell us, "This will happen and then this will happen and then it will work like this." We've got somebody coming from another country who tells us they have used this program in their country and it has been successful. It looks good, but we have not been eyewitnesses to it.

Tutor 2: So, what this comes down to is, we are asking teachers to trust us when we don't really trust ourselves.

Tutors found themselves learning as they were going, dealing with new content, new structures, and new roles at the very same moment that they were expected to teach others. In the months before school commitments were made, Tutors had been given some time to study and discuss *First Steps* among themselves, time to prepare for the teacher training sessions they would lead and the coaching and modeling they would do. However, they had little or no sustained opportunity to test out their interpretation of the literacy innovation with children before having to assume the role of "expert." They had little training in the skills of professional development beyond that offered in their Tutor training course, and once started in the field, they had minimal opportunity to work together to revise their hunches about what their roles should be.

Neither understanding nor accepting their status as neo-novices, the Tutors continuously set very high expectations for themselves. They became increasingly frustrated by their limited ability to effect change. These feelings were exacerbated by state and district pressures for quick results. Newspaper articles that consistently pointed the finger at hardworking teachers whose children did not achieve high test scores added yet another layer of frustration. The pressures to "get out there and make it work" resulted in a focus on outreach and activity.

The Teachers' Knowledge Base

In the early days of implementation Tutors came to see that a gap existed between the beliefs about teaching and learning held by individual teachers and beliefs that grounded the practices of *First Steps*. One teacher, speaking of the vision of good teaching dominant in her school, commented, "We are like a parochial school in the public sector. We like to be able to anticipate just what is going to happen in our class-rooms. And we want to keep it that way."

As a group, faculty members in this school had voiced their beliefs in child-centered pedagogy. However, in individual interviews, teachers spoke of their comfort with a fixed curriculum. They did not welcome the role of teacher as curriculum maker. It was these perspectives that Tutors and researchers alike found most evident in their classroom practices.

With the help of *First Steps*, teachers in this school did make signifi-cant changes in the ways in which they taught writing. Nonetheless, their instructional orientation invariably began with the text rather than with the child. Most had difficulty in seeing assessment and instruction as recursive processes. They accepted the *First Steps* premise that assess-ment should be linked to instruction. However, they interpreted this to mean that assessment should validate rather than inform instructional choices. The teachers not only needed support in implementing the ped-agogy of *First Steps* but also in understanding the theoretical paradigm on which these practices were based.

The Tutors had not been prepared to identify and meet teachers' needs in this area. They assumed that teachers who committed them-selves to the implementation not only agreed with *First Steps* beliefs but held a shared meaning of the implications of the beliefs for instructional practice. At first, Tutors thought teachers were simply being resistant to a deeper form of implementation. As they began to understand the complexity of the situation, they became even more concerned about how they should respond.

The Tutors' Knowledge Base

Those chosen to be district Tutors were highly respected, experienced professionals. Drawn from positions as reading resource teachers or monolingual or bilingual classroom teachers, all had strong literacy backgrounds in reading and/or writing. But the Tutors had only mini-mal experience with *First Steps* before they assumed their professional development responsibilities. Consequently, while they were all steeped in the literature of the innovation and deeply committed to it, the Tu-tors lacked a deep well of personal experience with *First Steps* on which to draw.

The Tutors quickly recognized that the teachers with whom they were working had different learning styles, different knowledge bases for literacy instruction, different visions of teaching and learning, and, consequently, different levels of comfort with the practices that *First Steps* was recommending. As master teachers, the Tutors knew how to work with students whose experiences, knowledge bases, and learning styles were diverse. They understood the meaning of resistance in children and knew ways in which to address it. They had not anticipated that they would be called upon to apply these skills to their work with their colleagues, and they were reluctant to do so.

Moreover, the Tutors believed that they should follow the articulated script for the conduct of professional development. In Tutor training sessions *First Steps* consultants had encouraged participants to adapt their training resources to meet the needs of local teachers. However, they did not show them how to do this. And in those same training sessions *First Steps* consultants had emphasized that specific pieces of information needed to be very clearly communicated to teachers. They consistently pointed out to Tutors that the materials in the Tutor resource book had been designed and sequenced with important goals in mind. To complicate the process even further, district administrators were leery of making modifications in a program whose presentations they had found so impressive.

The Tutors felt a tension between the desire to ensure programmatic integrity and the acknowledgment that training needed to be flexible. This tension, combined with their own limited experience in implementing *First Steps*, led them to feel as if they had little leeway in their use of the *First Steps* professional development methods and materials. They felt as if it was their role to disseminate the information they had received by adhering as closely as possible to the models they had observed during their own training.

Support for the Tutors

As the Tutors' workload increased and with it the amount of preparation they needed to do, Friday meetings that had been intended as a time for building a team approach to implementation were subordinated to the mechanics of getting plans and materials in order. This eased the immediate needs but deprived Tutors of the long-term benefits of more reflective practice.

The coordinator of reading to whom the Tutors reported was new to her own role in central office administration. Like the Tutors, she was frustrated by the enormity of her responsibilities and overextended by the ongoing requests for help that she was receiving from the 31 district schools. As a result, it was difficult for her to provide the steady leadership that would create a safe, supportive environment in which the Tutors might grow into their new roles.

Her efforts to make things work by trying different models of implementation were construed by the Tutors as obstacles to their efficacy. It seemed to them that their experiences in the field were not being taken into account, their voices were not being heard. The administrators were trying to be flexible, to identify unanticipated needs, and to develop responses to them in a timely way. But, to the Tutors, this "flexibility" was perceived as an obstacle to their efforts to engage meaningfully with teachers.

Tutors felt as if the ongoing relationships they had been working so hard to engender were being compromised by shifting assignments and schedules. They felt isolated, unsupported, and thoroughly inadequate. "I don't have the time, the energy, or the power to give teachers what would be most helpful." The Tutors felt that they had been let down and that they, in turn, were letting down their colleagues. By the end of the first year of our study, as teachers were beginning to feel more positively about the implementation process, the Tutors felt that the sense of possibility fueling their work was sorely diminished.

ANALYSIS

The teacher of teachers model of professional development is, in many ways, extremely compelling. The availability of in-district or in-house support personnel who will extend and support the knowledge base of their colleagues on an ongoing basis has both economic and ideological appeal. The cost of developing in-house expertise requires far less capital outlay than the utilization of outside expertise. In times of fiscal leanness the teacher of teachers model can be fiscally responsive to the needs of school districts. With a onetime expenditure for training, districts, in essence, avail themselves of renewable resources. In addition, the model makes it possible to custom-tailor the professional development experience to the needs of specific teachers by following up large and small group workshops with ongoing individual coaching (Joyce & Showers, 1995; Sparks & Loucks-Horsley, 1989). However, our findings suggest that the complexity of implementing a teacher of teachers model may well be significantly underestimated.

The literature reports that effective teachers of teachers possess a knowledge base both in the content of the program implementation and in the theory, skills, and strategies of professional development (Fullan, 1993; McLaughlin, 1991). When part of this knowledge base is new to the field or, as with *First Steps*, new to the professional developers as well as to the teachers, implementation is compromised. It takes time for those who serve as the teachers of teachers to develop the kinds of understanding that will make it possible for them to work effectively with their colleagues. All too often the time needed for this learning is underestimated. Rarely are the structures that are needed to support the learning of the professional development personnel provided or even acknowledged.

Many of the most salient problems that occurred during the initial phase of *First Steps* implementation were directly linked to the limited experience that Southtown Tutors had in both the specific content of the implementation and in the processes of professional development. District expectations that the Tutors, because they were master teachers, would be able to acquire needed information and experience quickly and independently exacerbated the situation.

The Tutors felt as if they were in over their heads, and they were. Where they were mistaken was in blaming themselves for the difficulties they encountered. Knowledge of how to work skillfully with children does not automatically transfer to work with adults. The Tutors needed time and support in order to learn how to help teachers move from transmission-oriented models of literacy instruction to inquiry-oriented models. The resources they were offered by *First Steps* and by district administrators were good, but they were not commensurate with the enormity of the charge.

At first glance, this finding seems paradoxical. The Tutors attended more than 8 days of in-depth training sessions sponsored by *First Steps*. They had time in spring of 1996 to prepare for their role as presenters of the introductory courses and to develop model lessons based on *First Steps* suggested practice. They had ongoing opportunities to meet and discuss issues of concern with *First Steps* consultants. However, a careful look at the literature on professional development and adult learning shows that despite all of these opportunities, there were important gaps in the ways in which they were prepared for the implementation process.

Joyce and Showers (1995) describe the complexity of introducing new visions of teaching into teachers' and trainers' existing repertoire of instructional strategies and the discomfort that results when these strategies conflict with preexisting strategies. Referring to the assumption commonly held by trainers and learners that observation of modeled strategies or processes is sufficient preparation for skillful and appropriate implementation, they point out the importance of opportunities for guided practice. They stress the need for teachers and teachers of teachers alike to have opportunities over time to try out their new learning, to receive constructive critique on their efforts, and to have time throughout the implementation process to reflect on and hone their practice.

The Tutors spent a great deal of time practicing their presentation skills and their model lessons. They did not, however, receive guided instruction or critical feedback from more expert colleagues on an ongoing basis. The assumption that their strong background knowledge of literacy would in itself be sufficient to enable them to communicate *First Steps* comfortably and effectively to their colleagues proved false; their related experience was helpful but not adequate. Their limited experience in implementing *First Steps* made it more difficult for them to demonstrate the connections between teachers' existing repertoire of instructional practices and the more inquiry-oriented approaches advocated by *First Steps*. Like the teachers with whom they were working, the Tutors could have benefited from actual "classroom assistance" over time in order to fully understand the philosophy and practice of *First Steps*.

Opportunities to participate in ongoing study groups also would have been helpful. There, encouraged to describe their work as teachers and learners, to identify the strands of connection that run through successful experiences, and to work together to develop a common vision, a common vocabulary, and a shared set of practices (Moll, 1997), they might have been able to grapple more effectively with their frustrations and anxiety. The opportunity for them to form such a group was available, but the leadership was missing—in part because it was not considered a priority and in part because the role of facilitator was never articulated or assigned.

The literature on school reform reports that the teacher plays a pivotal role in the change process. When teachers articulate a need or have a problem they are invested in solving, their desire to learn supports and sustains the change effort from within. Theoretically, the teacher of teachers model makes it possible to acknowledge and galvanize teacher strengths and concerns in timely ways. Known and respected by their colleagues, teachers of teachers bring credibility to their roles as professional developers. Common experiences, a common pool of knowledge, and familiarity with the values, expectations, and goals characterizing a particular school and district provide a basis for collaboration and dialogue from the very beginning of their tenure (Barkley, McCormick, & Taylor, 1987; Fullan with Stiegelbauer, 1991; Joyce & Showers, 1995). Our findings indicate that these ties were indeed beneficial to the Tutors in their new roles.

However, the literature of reform also documents that discrepancies between teachers' espoused beliefs and their actual teaching practices are quite common (Clark & Peterson, 1990; Hargreaves & Fullan, 1992; Little & McLaughlin, 1993). The Tutors were not prepared for these discrepancies. When they realized that despite the articulation of a districtwide vision of literacy instruction and the development and dissemination of clearly stated literacy goals and outcomes, many teachers implemented classroom practices that had no relation to these goals, they were stunned. Even more amazing to them was the discovery that significant numbers of teachers believed that, as district policy professed, they were enacting an integrated approach to the teaching of reading, writing and language arts, when in fact their practice consisted primarily of isolated skills instruction.

When invited into the classrooms of these teachers, Tutors found themselves unprepared to provide effective support. They had no wish to invoke the role of "expert," and yet they found that they had expertise that many of their colleagues did not. They felt prepared to engage in a "helping relationship"—a relationship in which an individual takes on the responsibility of promoting the growth, development, and improved functioning of the other (Rogers, 1961)—but felt their ability to do so was contingent upon their colleagues' abilities to identify their own needs. When teachers did not recognize the extent of their own needs, they feared they were working on a foundation of sand.

They knew how to work with children who had similar needs, but did not feel comfortable invoking this expertise in the context of professional development. They acknowledged learning was a lifelong process; they could identify the similarities between the needs of the teachers with whom they were working and the needs of the children with whom they had worked. However, they worried that it might be disrespectful to approach the learning process of their colleagues as they would that of children. For the most part, they lacked a background in the theory and practices of adult learning, and they did not find it within the training models for *First Steps* Tutors. Without this knowledge base they felt hamstrung.

Moreover, whereas they saw themselves as helping friends or collaborators with teachers in curriculum development, teachers preferred to defer to them in matters of curriculum design. They were often introduced to children as "the expert in writing." For many Tutors, these expectations were uncomfortable, making them feel fraudulent, exacerbating their already palpable anxiety, and compromising their own sense of agency. The absence of safe, structured contexts in which they might share their feelings with peers or more experienced personnel hampered their own professional growth and development and, by extension, that of the teachers with whom they worked.

Saxl, Lieberman, and Miles (1987) point out that professional development personnel need to be able to assume both stances, that of expert and that of helper. To be effective in both roles requires the development of a broad range of knowledge including skills in interpersonal relationships, group process, organizational strategies, trust building, and confrontation and conflict mediation as well as an understanding of content and access to resources. Those who serve in this role need to be judiciously selected and carefully trained in the myriad components of their job. Rarely is this done.

Barkley, McCormick and Taylor (1987) point out that training needs to continue over time. A team needs to be forged. Lines of communication among teachers of teachers need to be carefully constructed and kept open throughout the implementation process. Underlying all is the need to develop a relationship of mutual trust between professional development personnel and administrators and among professional development personnel themselves. Only then will they be able to engender an optimal environment for learning among the teachers with whom they work. Had these support structures been more carefully addressed in Southtown, had scheduled debriefing meetings focused initially on trust building and teamsmanship, the Tutors' sense of agency during the early stages of implementation might have been quite different.

CONCLUSION

The implementation of the teacher of teachers model in Southtown has proven to be much more complex than anyone had anticipated. And yet anecdotal and researched-based accounts of change suggest that the experiences of the Southtown Tutors are more the rule than the exception. What then are the implications of this study for those whose mission it is to help teachers move from transmission-oriented teaching to transactional and inquiry teaching? What do we contribute about the relationship between professional development and school change?

First of all, it was not merely a new set of materials and practices that teachers needed in order to link instruction and assessment but a new way of looking at their role as teachers—a new way of looking at self, a new way of looking at children. The Tutors had not realized that bringing about such changes, in essence a paradigm switch from transmission- to inquiry-oriented teaching, would be their responsibility. They never doubted that teachers who voiced agreement with district policy and the belief system of *First Steps* might not understand the pedagogical implications of their beliefs. All too often this is the reality that teachers of teachers encounter. For these models to be effective, it is essential that professional developers have opportunities to explore the big picture and develop strategies for helping teachers to change not only their instructional practices but the ways of thinking from which they emerge.

Second, the literature clearly documents that children and teachers need guided instruction if they are to fully internalize new information and strategies and apply them in a broad range of settings and experiences. Our findings extend the documentation of this need to the professional developers as well.

The literature also shows that for teachers and students change is a process that takes place over time. Our findings support the hypothesis that for teachers of teachers, the acquisition of the knowledge and skills needed to help others through the change process is also a process that takes time. It is not enough to provide professional development personnel with instructional opportunities and support groups in preparation for the implementation. These need to be provided on an ongoing basis throughout the implementation.

It is likely that all professional development personnel need to feel that they are part of a team in which teachers and administrators work together to make schools more effective learning environments. The challenges professional development personnel face are prodigious; there is no question but that feelings of isolation like those experienced by Southtown Tutors undermine effectiveness. Teachers of teachers, new to the professional development role, are in particular need of forums in which to discuss their new responsibilities and the challenges these involve, to problem solve, and to use each other as resources. In addition, they need practice that is guided and critiqued by someone whose expertise exceeds their own if they are to develop needed skills both in the content area in which they will be providing training and in the methodology they will be using to communicate this content.

Like all professional development roles, the role of teachers of teachers is complex. The data from Southtown clearly show that it cannot be assumed that the knowledge and experience teachers bring with them will transfer quickly or automatically to their new role as change agents. It is true that working with adults is in many ways analogous to working with children. However, the process needs to be carefully analyzed, strategies need to be learned, and theoretical underpinnings need to be understood if teachers of teachers are to be most effective.

The teacher of teachers model of professional development holds great promise for the field, but it is no quick fix. If teachers of teachers are to help teachers make change—especially change from transmission-oriented teaching to inquiry-oriented teaching—the research suggests that the same kinds of experiences and supports must be in place for them that it is hoped they will put in place for the teachers with whom they work.

REFERENCES

Allington, R. (1997). Message from the president. *National Reading Conference Yearbook*. Chicago: National Reading Conference.

Barkley, W., McCormick, W., & Taylor, R. (1987). Teachers as workshop leaders: A model for teachers training teachers. *Journal of Staff Development*, 8(2), 45–47.

Clandinin, D. J., & Connelly, F. M. (1995). *Teachers' professional knowledge landscapes*. New York: Teachers College Press.

Clark, C., & Peterson, P. (1990). Teachers' thought processes. In M. C. Wittrock (Ed.), *Handbook of research on teaching* (pp. 297–314). New York: Macmillan.

Cochran-Smith, M., & Lytle, S. L. (Eds.). (1993). *Inside/outside: Teacher research and knowledge*. New York: Teachers College Press.

Darling-Hammond, L. (1998). Teachers and teaching: Testing policy hypotheses from a national commission report. *Educational Researcher*, 27(1), 5–15.

Education Department of Western Australia. (1996). *First Steps*. Melbourne, Australia: Addison Wesley Longman Australia Pty LTD.

Fullan, M. (1993). *Change forces*. Philadelphia: Falmer Press.

Fullan, M. (with Stiegelbauer, S.). (1991). *The new meaning of educational change*. New York: Teachers College Press.

Hargreaves, A. (1996). Revisiting voice. *Educational Researcher*, 25(1), 12–19.

Hargreaves, A., & Fullan, M. G. (1992). *Understanding teacher development*. New York: Teachers College Press.

Joyce, B., & Showers, B. (1995). *Student achievement through staff development*. White Plains, NY: Longman.

Lieberman, A. (Ed.). (1988). *Building a professional culture in schools*. New York: Teachers College Press.

Lieberman, A., & Miller, L. (Eds.). (1991). *Staff development for education in the '90s: New demands, new realities*. New York: Teachers College Press.

Little, J. W., & McLaughlin, M. W. (1993). *Teachers' work: Individuals, colleagues, and contexts*. New York: Teachers College Press.

Loucks-Horsely, S., & Stiegelbauer, S. (1991). Using knowledge of change to guide staff development. In A. Lieberman & L. Miller (Eds.), *Staff devel-*

opment for education in the '90s (pp. 15–36). New York: Teachers College Press.

McLaughlin, M. W. (1991). Enabling professional development. In A. Lieberman & L. Miller (Eds.), *Staff development for education in the '90s* (pp. 61–82). New York: Teachers College Press.

Moll, L. (1997). The creation of mediating settings. *Mind, culture and activity.* Los Angeles: Regents of the University of California on behalf of the Laboratory of Comparative Human Cognition.

Moll, L. (1999, June). *Funds of knowledge: Rethinking culture and schooling.* Keynote address presented at the conference *Beyond Tomorrow: Issues in Urban Literacy,* Bank Street College of Education, New York.

Peterson, P. (1998). Why do educational research? Rethinking our roles and identities, our texts and contexts. *Educational researcher, 27*(3), 4–10.

Putnam, R., & Borko, H. (2000). What do new views of knowledge and thinking have to say about research on teaching learning? *Educational Research, 29*(1), 4–15.

Rogers, C. (1961). *On becoming a person.* Boston: Houghton Mifflin

Saxl, E., Lieberman, A., & Miles, M. (1987). Help is at hand: New knowledge for teachers as staff developers. *Journal of Staff Development, 8*(1), 7–11.

Sparks, D., & Loucks-Horsley, S. (1989). Five models of staff development for teachers. *Journal of Staff Development, 10*(4), 40–57.

Vygotsky, L. (1978). *Mind in society: The development of higher psychological processes* (M. Cole, V. John-Steiner, S. Scribner, & E. Souberman, Eds.). Cambridge, MA: Harvard University Press. (Original work published 1922–1935)

Chapter 4

Partners in School Innovation: An Unusual Approach to Change Facilitation

Kim Grose

The professional development of teachers is a critical component of educational reform processes. Much of the professional literature over the past 2 decades recognizes the value of site-based, flexible, and ongoing support for teacher learning within the process of institutional reform (Hall & Hord, 1987; Lieberman, 1995; McLaughlin, 1991). Moreover, there is increasing recognition that "although teachers spend most of their time facilitating for student learning, they themselves have few people facilitating for them and understanding their need to be recognized, encouraged, helped, supported, and engaged in professional learning" (Lieberman, Saxl, & Miles, 1988, p. 152).

In 1993 colleague Julien Phillips and I founded an organization called Partners in School Innovation that responded to this need. It was based on two primary assumptions: (1) Public schools had to reform substantially in order to meet the needs of low-income children and children of color, and (2) well-prepared young college graduates could be valuable resources to teachers in achieving such reform. Within 5 years we saw schools make strides in meeting unmet student needs, and we saw the Partners serve as valuable change facilitators.

This chapter describes the work and experiences of this unusual kind of change facilitator, one without formal authority or educational expertise. It points to some emerging ideas about broadening the notion of who can facilitate school reform work and teacher development, what these change facilitators can contribute, and what support they need. It also raises questions for further inquiry about what challenges their position poses and how diversity of culture and personal experience influences both the experience of such change facilitators and the contributions they make to the schools in which they work.

I write this as a practitioner. Although trained as an anthropologist, I assembled these data between 1994 and 1998 not as a formal participant-observer but as a participant, pure and simple, who questioned, reflected, and read.

THE ORGANIZATION

Partners in School Innovation is a nonprofit organization founded in 1993 to support whole-school change efforts in public schools serving low-income communities across the San Francisco Bay Area. It commits to partnerships of 3–5 years with elementary and middle schools that have begun the process of whole-school change, that have articulated clear goals and identified strategies for moving forward, and that are ready to use the support that the Partners initiative can provide. This support consists primarily of teams of diverse, college-educated Ameri-Corps members who serve literally as partners alongside teachers in implementing innovative change projects that are the building blocks for schoolwide reform.

The organization seeks to involve in school reform a broad range of people who share the vision that educational change can increase equity and community in our society (Freire, 1970; Meier, 1995). It works to help schools ensure the positive development and achievement of low-income children and children of color. We choose to work with schools serving this population because we want to dispel the overwhelming societal assumptions that such children cannot achieve (Gonzalez et al., 1993). Schools that have made a commitment to educate poor and minority children to high levels are most in need of intensive and creative support, and their success, we believe, can have the most impact on the public school system as a whole.

Teams of Partners currently work with seven schools in five different school districts in the Bay Area. This corps of 27 Partners (we started with 9) includes recent college graduates from around the United States. They are selected through a rigorous application process, bringing a commitment to children, a track record of leadership and involvement in their communities, and strong communication and interpersonal skills. They commit to 2 years of service and are paid a yearly stipend of $15,000. They also receive educational vouchers through AmeriCorps worth close to $5,000 for each year of service. Among the Partners there is a wide range of cultural, ethnic, socioeconomic, and academic backgrounds. The organization deliberately seeks Partners with diverse interests, backgrounds, and experiences, including teaching and education reform, community organizing, social service work, advocacy, and research. This follows from our assumption that schools are important democratic institutions in their local communities and will benefit from change facilitators and staff members who may not be career educators, but who will broaden educational dialogue with their own questions and perspectives (Delpit, 1989; Gonzalez et al., 1993; Nieto, 1996).

The history of education reform shows that educators at all levels participate in workshops in "best practices," but rarely have the ongoing support to integrate these new practices into their day-to-day lives in the school—as principals, teachers, or other school personnel. They are even less likely to spread the knowledge to others in a sustained way (Lieberman, 1995; McLaughlin, 1991). Partners in School Innovation set out to support educators at the crucial juncture between first exposure and deep practice. Its design rests on the following theories of action:

- *Partners are full members of the school staff.* Working in a school 4 days per week, Partners are able to gain a deep understanding of the complexity of the particular school change process (Fullan, 1993), the institutional context or situation in which teachers are learning and implementing changes (McLaughlin, 1991; Putnam & Borko, 2000), and the funds of knowledge that the teachers, students, families, and others bring to this context (Moll & Greenberg, 1990). With such understanding they are able to provide support that is guided by the particular needs of the people going through the changes (Loucks-Horsely & Stiegelbauer, 1991).

- *Partners work as peers of teachers, not as assistants or authorities.* Because they are not in positions of authority over teachers and do not come into schools as experts, Partners are able to engage with teachers about their practice without threatening the "safe place" that teachers value in their classrooms (Clandinin & Connelly, 1995). Eventually, through their work with teachers and the reflective questions they ask, they are able to help teachers revisit and hone their practices (Lee & Barnett, 1994).

- *Partners are insider-outsiders.* In addition to being full members of a school staff and community, they are part of an outside network of other Partners and educational organizations, and receive ongoing external training. As outsiders, they can utilize the resources of the broader community. With training and experience, they can bring students, families, and others into the reform process. Additionally, they are supported by their outside organization in raising questions—for example, about expectations for students and issues of equity—that are often difficult to raise from within (Fullan, 1993).

• *Partners work on integrated projects as part of a whole school reform process.* Projects are high-leverage reform activities, identified and led collaboratively by Partners and teacher colleagues that can move practitioners from initial experimentation to deep practice (Sparks & Hirsch, 1997). Through careful and ongoing project management, Partners and teachers learn together how to assess what is needed, how to implement a new practice or innovation on a small scale, and how to engage in a cycle of inquiry around the experiment through several iterations (Fullan, 1993). In this way they deepen the experiment with a base of knowledge and experience in-house, develop increasing ownership and vision across the school community, and manage the implementation and expansion of the innovation in a way tailored to the needs and culture of the site (Fullan, 1993; McLaughlin, 1991).

• *Given specific support and training, Partners facilitate whole-school change.* Much like the nonprincipal change facilitator described by Hall & Hord (1987) as a "consigliere," Partners take care of the logistics of implementing an innovation, do individual problem solving and reflection with teachers, communicate across the school, strategize with the principal, develop materials and trainings, find resources, respond to concerns, and, above all, ask questions. Both "on the job" and through ongoing training, coaching, and reflection provided by Partners in School Innovation, Partners learn many of the same skills that resource teachers learn as they become coaches and change facilitators. These include how to build trusting relationships, diagnose individual and organizational needs, manage a change process, find and use resources, plan strategically, and build the skill and confidence of others (Lieberman et al., 1988).

THE STORY OF PARTNERSHIPS IN TWO SCHOOLS

By 1998 Partners in School Innovation had worked with two of its partner schools for close to 5 years. During that time, 2–3 teams of Partners had cycled through each school. At each site many different projects were launched, experimented with, and dropped or expanded as part of their evolving school-change process and because of changing priorities, lessons, and leadership. These two elementary schools (whose names have been changed here) stand as examples of the actual work of Partners with children, teachers, principals, and the communities. They also reflect significant differences in context and role for Partners.

The first school, which is very large, has a long history of reform through a highly democratic process with participation from multiple school and community stakeholders. The Partners there were put to use quickly by school leaders and teachers who knew how to use resources effectively and who routinely welcomed nonteaching staff into their school community. An ongoing challenge in the partnership was how to locate the change facilitation resource of Partners at the heart of the school's reform work. Several school projects that Partners worked on were well-supported by teachers and administrators (these are described below). Others got lost among the many innovations and reform priorities at work simultaneously across the 60+ classrooms, and eventually Partners ended their support of those innovations.

The second school described (Webster Academy) launched its partnership with Partners in School Innovation at the same time that it opened. Both parties to the partnership began with a strong sense of mutual ownership and collaboration. "Partners started the school with us" was a common refrain of the principal. In a small school with a strong principal and a clear, focused whole-school-change goal of increasing literacy, Partners in School Innovation did not have difficulty situating the support of their Partners at the core of the reform work, at least at the broad level of overall goals and plans. The challenge on the ground for the Partners was in finding ways to translate these goals and plans into tangible support for teachers. This proved difficult since the two main strategies endorsed by the principal for achieving the schoolwide goal were assessment and action research, areas in which few of the teachers or Partners had either experience or commitment. The Partners also found it challenging to help bridge the gap between a largely White, young, middle-class faculty and an overwhelmingly low-income, Latino student and family community.

Hillcrest Elementary School

Collectively, the children at this large urban school speak more than 17 languages; 88 percent receive free or reduced-price lunch. Parents, teachers, and others in the community have come together frequently in recent years to address their concerns about low reading test scores (average 20th percentile) and to focus the school's reform efforts increasingly on literacy. In some years Partners were more connected into schoolwide reform initiatives than in other years, and there was a continual process of review and negotiation with the principal, the leadership team of the school, and various teacher colleagues over how the school could make best use of the change facilitation resource they had. Between 1994 and 1995 the school leadership team and Partners in School Innovation agreed to pursue two collaborative reform projects: (a) the introduction of a literacy strategy called "Reciprocal Teaching" (Palinscar & Brown, 1984) and (b) an initiative to engage parents in the literacy development of their children.

Reciprocal Teaching. This is a structured teaching strategy for reading comprehension that involves children working together in small groups to make meaning out of text using four explicit strategies: prediction, summary, clarifying questions, and "teacher" questions. After initial introduction to the strategies and some practice with a teacher or other trained person, students eventually run their own "RT" groups: They learn to learn from and support one another.

In the first year, Partners were trained in the practice and helped four pioneering teachers, fourth through sixth grade, to make Reciprocal Teaching an integral part of their ongoing curriculum. The teachers were intrigued with Reciprocal Teaching and were interested in pursuing it in their classrooms both to build reading comprehension skills and critical thinking in students who were scoring well below grade level and to change the dynamics in the classroom to more collaborative learning. The Partners worked alongside the teachers in the classroom with small groups of children and collected formal and informal data on the implementation of the strategy. They discussed their observations with teachers during lunch and after school. During regular progress reviews, they compiled and summarized data about both the process of implementation and the learning of the students. For example, they were able to point out particular students who had been unable to grasp stories on their own, but in the group asked good questions and summarized well.

When the teachers became convinced that the strategy was addressing their students' needs, the challenge for the Partners became one of managing a major expansion of the program and institutionalizing the effort while continuing to deepen the practice. How could they scale it up to become a routine schoolwide practice that was understood and used in the majority of more than 60 classrooms?

Over the course of 3 years Partners served as project managers and trainers. Using collaboratively developed 1-year objectives as their guides and frequently checking in with the lead teachers, the Partners figured out various strategies to expand Reciprocal Teaching. They trained students and teachers, recruited and trained volunteers to support Reciprocal Teaching in the classrooms, developed a guide and video, created a resource library of materials for students and teachers, observed teachers in their classrooms and provided feedback, facilitated teacher discussions on the range of ways to use the strategy, led strategic planning of the project's expansion, and collected assessment on student performance and process data on the implementation effort.

After 3 years Reciprocal Teaching had spread to 26 classrooms, reaching over 800 students each year. Hillcrest made Reciprocal Teaching the subject of ongoing schoolwide professional development and reflection. To sustain the practice, Partners and teachers organized a cadre of older, experienced students to provide focused training in new classrooms. A former Partner, who became the Hillcrest reform coordinator, commented:

> I have noticed a major shift in how much Reciprocal Teaching is a part of the fabric of the school. It was a tiny experiment when I got here 3 years ago; now it is taken for granted as something that happens at Hillcrest. The bigger questions that we are all still asking are how can we ensure that teachers are practicing the spirit and the letter, that the ideas behind the practice—not just the activity—are being transferred and deepened. (CJ, 1/18/98)

Other Literacy Projects. The second major project at Hillcrest sought to engage parents in literacy projects with their children and the school. Over 2 years, one Partner took the lead in developing a menu of activities: schoolwide family literacy events; monthly classroom-based workshops called "Home-School Connections"; family homework activities; and an ESL readers program that brought adult English-language learners into primary-grade classrooms to read with children in English and talk about their immigrant experiences.

Unlike the Reciprocal Teaching project in which a specific teaching approach had been identified and agreed upon, this project emerged from a challenge—how to engage parents as partners in improving literacy. The Partner reflected on this challenge:

> I had to help teachers move from a disempowered, hopeless place of inaction, in which they were complaining and unable to see what they could do, to a place where they could be active about

it. That maybe things wouldn't be perfect but you could keep trying and fine tune things. (LT, 1/18/98)

Experimental and entrepreneurial, this initiative was built on the interests of teachers who volunteered to try things out, and with the strategic, logistical, and facilitative support of the lead Partner.

Initially, the Partner had to feel her way; through outside field research and careful questioning, listening, and practice, she engaged teachers and parents in the experiment. Advertising at staff meetings her availability to support teachers in working with parents on literacy, she would then arrange one-on-one or small-group meetings with interested teachers. There she would listen to their concerns and ideas and share the practices she had helped other teachers develop. They would agree on ways to work together. Later, as certain practices built momentum, she facilitated meetings with multiple teachers planning a schedule of parent-teacher activities. Eventually she helped teachers to plan and facilitate the meetings and activities themselves.

Two years later, when this lead Partner moved on in her career, the leadership team of the school agreed to continue the most valued activities. The teachers had not only acquired new skills and knowledge about how to involve parents in literacy efforts, but they had made sense of the knowledge in their own context, integrating the practices into their way of doing things.

Webster Academy

Webster Academy is located in a low-income neighborhood of an otherwise wealthy suburban town. Of about 400 students at this public elementary school, 67 percent speak Spanish as their home language; 89 percent receive free or reduced-price lunch. The school is organized into multigraded classrooms with teams of two or three teachers sharing students. Concerned about low literacy scores, the school has set explicit grade-level benchmarks and standards for its students, and, in accord with state mandates, reduced its student-teacher ratio in the primary grades to 20:1.

At Hillcrest, Partners worked as managers of the implementation and expansion of projects that involved teachers in the classroom and beyond. At Webster Academy, the Partners took on a different kind of role, becoming close colleagues of teachers in a schoolwide assessment initiative. Their primary work was to collect and analyze reading data and facilitate teacher dialogue regarding the meaning and implications of the data.

The challenges the Partners faced in this initiative included the following: how to support an entire school in developing a system for regular assessment and analysis; how to build a culture of inquiry about literacy instruction using student data; and how to bring new and inexperienced teachers into what sometimes felt like a "mandated" reform process. The Partners also struggled with their own personal concerns, namely, how to build credibility with teachers when they themselves had little to no teaching or assessment experience and whether focusing on data collection and analysis would have any positive consequences for student learning.

Partners invested heavily in their own learning through reading, district trainings, observation and practice in classrooms, and dialogue with teachers and the school's literacy coach. They also spent a good deal of time talking with one another, finding their team to be a place to voice concerns and struggles and to gain needed personal support. At the same time, they worked with primary teachers to build the teachers' capacity in the area of assessment.

Over the course of the first year, Partners conducted literacy assessments with children, including running records, letter identification, and print awareness tasks; collected and compiled data amassed by the teachers; made initial analyses; and facilitated teaching-team meetings. By being in the classroom a significant amount of time, they were able to informally observe teachers and give feedback. They asked countless questions in the context of conversations with teachers about students and learning. Their focus was to create opportunities for teachers to analyze and discuss one another's data, and to develop action research questions and instructional experiments.

By year's end all 12 primary teachers had accomplished the school's expectation of implementing assessments at regular intervals for all children and using individual student assessment data in some way to inform instructional decisions.

At the primary level, where the goal was reading fluency for students, the school leadership had determined some schoolwide assessment tools that readily provided teachers with useful data about their students' fluency. But the process of assessment was vaguer at the upper-elementary level, where the concerns were more broadly defined as reading comprehension and English-language development. Teachers reluctantly conducted assessments without a clear sense of the relevance of the data to their instruction or their concerns.

By midyear Partners realized that they needed to work with the upper-grade teachers to investigate and identify assessments that would give them more valuable data for teaching reading comprehension and

for effectively helping children to make the transition from Spanish instruction into English.

> We wasted a lot of time and effort this year trying to work with
> teachers on assessments when most teachers did not want to be
> working with us on this. Now that we have allowed teachers to
> collectively choose what they wanted to work with us on in the ar-
> eas of literacy and data collection, we are making infinitely more
> progress. Teachers now stay long after meetings are supposed to
> end; they approach us to talk about the project, they offer sugges-
> tions about the work we can do together, and they voluntarily
> take on additional projects. (Partners End-Year Report, June
> 1997)

Complicating the work and efficacy of Partners were the cultural
differences between a largely White, middle-class school faculty and a
largely low-income Latino student community. The Partners, in particular those from backgrounds similar to the children, struggled with their
sense of loyalty and commitment to the teachers, who were often new
to the profession and overwhelmed by the low literacy skills of the students, and their feelings of anger and disappointment when teachers
vented their frustrations by blaming the students and their families.

During the annual partnership renegotiation process, several plans
for further learning and initiative emerged from this intense—and
sometimes conflict-filled—year. These plans included an action research group for teachers on second-language learning and appropriate
transition strategies; an agreement among upper-grade teachers to experiment with various comprehension assessments for gathering information on their students' progress; and a public engagement project
that brought parents into conversations about reading standards and
strategies and gave them opportunities to voice concerns and questions.

THE ROLE OF PARTNERS

These projects flourished, deepened, and grew over several years because they were clearly focused and articulated, and had significant
sponsorship and investment from teachers and ongoing support from
the principal. But what did Partners accomplish in these two schools
and others? First, simply because they were full-time additional staff,
they were able to extend and deepen what teachers were doing, increase
the rate at which change could occur, and enable school people to see

results more quickly. The Partners at Webster Academy enabled the teachers to have assessment data on all their students the first fall that it was required, something they would have been unable to complete on their own. Because the teachers had help, they were able to look at the data and work with it that winter. Recognizing its value, they continued the assessments themselves for the rest of the year. Similarly, the teachers at Hillcrest had been used to holding one or two classroom events a year for the parents of their students, but would not have been able to organize and manage monthly events without a Partner's help. The increased frequency of events enhanced communication between teachers and parents and in some cases deepened their relationships.

Second, the tasks Partners accomplished were not isolated and discrete; they were explicitly linked to whole-school change strategies. The Partners were extensively trained and supported by Partners in School Innovation to make these links. Through frequent and informal dialogues with teachers and administrators, Partners could raise long-term questions. Through regularly held, in-depth partnership reviews, the Partners, the director from Partners in School Innovation, the principal, and key school colleagues came together to discuss progress in the context of larger school goals.

Making this link was not easy, however. Both school colleagues and Partners have had to learn how to balance strategic thinking with pragmatic action, and give new members of the partnership time to learn. With the built-in turnover of Partners every 2 years (or less if a Partner chose not to return for a 2nd year), things did not always get off the ground quickly in the fall as new Partners were getting acclimated to their jobs. In these cases, some teachers found it frustrating that another group of new Partners was asking questions and doing their own "inquiry" when the teachers had gone through it all with the old Partners the year before. Similarly, when a Partnership director left and a new one began (as happened for some partnerships each year), it meant that built-up understanding and trust between this person and the principal was lost.

Partners learned from these experiences. At Webster, they learned that teachers needed help in analyzing their own data.

> By doing some initial analysis of data and coming up with some questions beforehand, we were able to engage teachers in more specific and targeted discussions that led to more changes in instructional practices. (Partners End-Year Report, June 1997)

They also learned how to navigate conflicts between organizational priorities that focused on long-term objectives and appeared to be in conflict with school colleagues' wishes to get immediate value from the additional people on-site.

Finally, they learned to trust the review process developed by their own organization. Frequent reviews of progress enabled project colleagues to get together and revise objectives and plans based on what had happened, what had not happened, and what they were learning (Fullan, 1993).

WHAT MAKES PARTNERSHIPS WORK IN THE REFORM PROCESS?

What light does the experience of Partners in School Innovation shed on the broader issues of change facilitation? What distinctive value might a change facilitator such as a Partner bring, and how can this experience broaden the field of possibilities for educational reform? The data indicate that Partners are able to influence change in at least three ways. First, they help teachers bridge the gap between initial learning and deep practice. Second, their work helps shift the learning paradigm in the schools from one of transmission from expert to learner to one of mutual coconstruction of learning and knowledge. Third, through who they are, the questions they raise, and the projects they focus on, Partners challenge schools on issues of equity.

These data confound the commonsense assumption that one needs to have deep knowledge of and experience in schools in order to effectively influence change. Why then are Partners successful? The data suggest that it is because (a) they have effective support structures for their own learning and work, (b) they leverage their insider-outsider status, and (c) they draw on a wide array of funds of knowledge. Finally, they are successful, in some ways, precisely because they do *not* have formal authority or expertise.

Supplying Informal Leadership

Partners are able to play change facilitation roles because their positions and support structures are set up according to what research over the years has shown to be effective for building professional learning communities: They are site based; their work is flexible depending on the priorities and needs of people in the school; they engage in collaborative action and learning; and they profit from the network of people inside and outside the school who are in similar positions (Lieberman, 1995; Lieberman et al., 1988; McLaughlin, 1991; Miller, 1988).

Working regularly with teachers in their classrooms and knowing the students well enabled Partners to help teachers bridge the gap between initial learning and deep practice. In multiple ways they contributed to the development of "discourse communities" (Putnam & Borko, 2000) that placed teaching and learning at the center of conversations between adults in the school. One Partner, who facilitated teachers talking together about their reading instruction, believed that these regular reflection groups helped teachers integrate information and ideas they had been exposed to in outside settings: "These small groups helped the formal staff development work for people with different individual styles" (BJ, 1/23/98)

Building Collegial Relationships

Partners in School Innovation, the schools, and individuals are trying to make a paradigm shift away from old models of school improvement, in which learning is conceived of as discrete, known, and transferred from teacher to learner. Reform in these schools assumes new roles and relationships for those involved and is based on the presumption that learning is coconstructed and emerges from practice (McLaughlin, 1991; Putnam & Borko, 2000; Sparks & Hirsch, 1997).

One of the difficulties in creating collegial coaching and learning relationships between teachers and change leaders is the assumption built into the educational system that experts tell others what or how to do things (Clandinin & Connolly, 1995; Lieberman, 1995). Partners are neither experts nor supervisors. They use reflective questioning and basic relationship-building skills to enable teachers to enter into dialogue about teaching without feeling judged (Lee & Barnett, 1994).

This paradigm shift is not easy for change facilitator or teacher. Partners operate right at the growing edge of their colleagues' development.

> Being a nonexpert helped because teachers feel like nonexperts, especially with parents. So having someone like me around showed teachers that you can do it and not have some super knowledge about it. It was difficult, too, because teachers *do* want an expert to tell them what to do. I couldn't prove to them that the ideas we had would work. I tried to explain that it was an experiment for the school and that I couldn't give answers. (LT, 1/18/98)

The Partners' nonexpert position is, paradoxically, an asset. Without the formal credibility of a teaching credential and experience that other change facilitators bring in with them, Partners had to work to build credibility. They learned to build collegial peer relationships with teachers in order to accomplish their work, and in doing so they created "safe" spaces for inquiry and reflection (Clandinin & Connolly, 1995) as well as new patterns of interaction and learning essential for reform (Fullan, 1993).

Interviews with Partners showed that the position of nonauthority enabled them to create opportunities for the teachers to pursue their authentic interests and deepen their practice. It also led to explicit questioning of the relationship between authority and change.

> It meant that when I recruited teachers to get involved in the project, they really wanted to. Working with people who are there voluntarily means you can go deeper with them. But you may be trading off breadth. What about the teachers who aren't doing the strategy and should be? But, then, can you force them to do it even with authority? (CJ, 1/18/98)

Developing Learning Opportunities

In working together with teachers and facilitating dialogue about what questions and ideas were emerging from the work, Partners helped create ongoing "learning opportunities that engage [teachers] in experiencing, creating, and solving real problems, using their own experiences and working with others" (Lieberman, 1995, p. 595).

At Webster Academy, for example, the Partners and teachers worked together and built their own culture of inquiry. Being a full-time resource meant that they could get to know the children well and be authentic coworkers with the teachers in ways that are not possible for someone coming in less frequently. "It established me as a member of the team, responsible for what happened and invested in the students" (BJ, 1/23).

Of course, there were experts—reform coordinators, literacy coaches, administrators, and external staff developers. The Partners worked on teams with them thus helping support the creation in the schools of new norms for relationships and learning that contributed to the school "reculturing" (Fullan, 1993).

Drawing on the trust and knowledge they had as insiders and gaining support from Partners in School Innovation, Partners also learned to raise questions in nonthreatening ways in their schools that others may not have been able to do. They benefited personally and professionally from an external institutional context that provided access to information, resources, and broader ideas about educational change (McDonald, 1989). In weekly meetings at Partners in School Innovation they had a space for grappling with complex issues of the role of education in social change and for raising questions as to who was successful in school and why.

> Professional development at Partners helped me constantly to push myself to make sure that children of color and their families were being served by the reform strategies at our school. We were supported by the organization in asking the questions, "Are kids of color being served? Why or why not? What strategies can we learn to better meet their needs?" Many teachers appreciated that I, or other Partners, raised these questions even though they were difficult ones to talk about. (HJ, 3/25/98)

Thus they were able to leverage both their insider and their outsider status to challenge schools on difficult topics, in particular, equity.

Using Available Resources

The funds of knowledge that Partners drew on to play their roles were extensive and varied. Three main areas of knowledge and experience stand out across the two schools described above and others. First, teachers and principals frequently commented positively about the organizational, planning, and facilitation skills of the Partners. Most Partners came in with some prior experience planning student conferences, running meetings, and organizing events. They also learned strategic action-planning and meeting-facilitation skills through Partners in School Innovation.

Second, many incoming Partners had substantial prior knowledge about school reform theory and practices, though all learned about major approaches and models through the organization. For example, of the eight Partners on the Hillcrest and Webster Academy teams in 1996–97, two Partners had worked at Brown University with Theodore Sizer and member schools of his Coalition of Essential Schools; two others had studied bilingual education policies and strategies in college. This background in theory and policy helped their credibility and confidence.

Third, many Partners had personal connections and prior experience with immigrant communities and communities of color. Six of the eight Partners at Hillcrest and Webster were people of color or had experience working in educational settings with Latino or Asian children. Most spoke Spanish. This provided them with a level of comfort among students and families that was much appreciated by school colleagues and families. This diversity also was of institutional value. It allowed opportunities for change initiatives and learning to emerge that may not have with a more homogeneous staff.

One major limitation in the funds of knowledge and experience that Partners generally brought was in the area of change management. Only a few had prior experience working in an environment of major change or had other knowledge of change models and practices. They received explicit training and support in change management that equipped them to some degree to operate within a change environment. However, as a whole the professional development program for Partners did not distinguish between the levels of concern (Loucks-Horsley & Stiegelbauer, 1991) that individuals had at different times concerning their change environment and the role they had within it.

Partners in School Innovation set up a number of structures to support the Partners' learning and development. They included 2 weeks of intensive pretraining, weekly 1-day professional development, monthly reflection with action research teams, 6-month performance appraisals, a team structure, collaborative work projects, and 3-day retreats twice each year. These structures provided opportunities for reflection with people in similar roles engaged in similar struggles. They also provided information and skill development so that Partners could do their job better. Through performance appraisals and on-site coaching from staff, Partners also received feedback on their work performance.

The exact form and content of these structures were fluid, changing each year depending on the creativity, needs, interests, and experience of the Partners and staff in any given year. Key areas of skill development, in which the organization developed increasing expertise, were the initial inquiry process into a new school community or a new project area; project management, including action planning and regular progress reviews with key colleagues; meeting preparation and facilitation; leadership development; and leveraging resources, especially students. As the Hillcrest and Webster Academy examples demonstrate, these skills were essential for Partners to be able to conduct their work.

I can do what I do because those are the expectations. The organization believes that I can play this role, and supports me to meet those expectations. I am not sure how they do it in a structural way, but I know that individuals at all levels support me individually in doing the job. It manifests itself in a lot of ways, by a staff person being on the other end of the phone when I need help with understanding some data, or by responding to my feedback and modifying reflection. (TK, 1/23/98)

The training could not, however, meet all needs. The relative inexperience built into the Partners model had consequences not only for the schools but also for the Partners themselves, who bore the brunt of the frustrations that their inexperience inevitably caused. Partners who were asked to support teachers in a particular literacy strategy, for example, found themselves heavily influenced by the attitudes of the collaborating teachers. If the teachers were confident and motivated, so were the Partners; however, in situations where the teachers expressed frustration and dragged their feet, the Partners had little prior experience to draw on to express support for the strategy or to motivate others. The programwide training structures of Partners in School Innovation could not provide the kind of detailed, school-specific information that these Partners often felt they wanted, and even the most supportive staff coaching or cross-team problem solving could not substitute for lived experience.

Reflections

The professional literature is replete with discussions of the problem of isolation in the teaching profession (Clandinin & Connolly, 1995; McLaughlin & Yee, 1988). The Partners discovered that change facilitation can also be isolating work because there may be few people, if any, in similar positions on-site, because the work is global in nature, and because it is often overwhelming.

The most significant support mentioned by the Partners was having teammates—other people who understood the school culture and the project work, who knew one another well, and who were in the same insider-outsider, nonexpert position. Also highly valued were the relationships with Partner colleagues in other schools:

The network of Partners wasn't extremely useful in terms of the specific work I was doing. But being able to talk with others about the successes and frustrations was helpful: to know others' experiences and realize it wasn't just my work that was hard. (BJ, 1/23/98)

Partners agreed that key support factors within the schools themselves included having "allies" in the school community that valued a project and wanted to be involved, and a school environment that welcomed and valued people in nonteaching roles.

> It felt good that people were coming to us to get involved, that we were helping people who wanted it. Also, the culture of the school was one that welcomed people in odd roles. There were lots of nonteacher people around, and that was OK. Teachers did not see them as taking away from the classroom, but as part of a team to provide support for students. (CJ, 1/18/98)

Some of the primary lessons Partners learned in their unusual and often stressful positions were that change happens slowly and there may not be a "right way" to contribute to school or social change. Instead they must hold the uncertainty in their minds while continuing to work. "It has been a humbling experience. I realize that you never get to the point where you've got the right answer" (GL, 1/23/98).

They also learned the importance of listening to others (Lieberman et al., 1988).

> It is really hard to quiet yourself down and just listen. Listen to [teachers'] concerns and what they want to work on. Then you can help them change, rather than pushing your own ideas. People need to be ready to listen to you and what you have to say. I realized that listening to others doesn't have to change how you feel. It can just expand your view because you hear others' views. (GL, 1/23/98)

CHALLENGES AND QUESTIONS FOR FURTHER STUDY

In this chapter, I have outlined some of what Partners in School Innovation has learned in its first 5 years. Of course, there remain areas to explore and questions to answer.

Insider/Outsider Roles

First, the structure of the Partner role—insider-outsiders without prior educational expertise who serve for 2 years in a school—has all the advantages and constraints described above. The organization invests heavily each fall in the new corps members, helping them in a crash course in school reform, team building, facilitation, project management, and their particular project area. The schools similarly invest in their learning about the particular school culture, people, history, and norms.

> It is frustrating how much time it takes to become a successful Partner. Just when you figure it out, it's over. The 2nd year the work is so much deeper and with greater impact, but you couldn't have skipped over the 1st year. It is just hard to have it be over. (CJ, 1/18/98)

The Challenge of Diversity

The second challenge arises from the organization's deliberate commitment to building a cadre of change facilitators with a range of personal and professional interests, experience, and backgrounds. The question of how one's background and prior experience influence one's efficacy as a change facilitator has scarcely been addressed in the educational literature. School reform processes and individuals gain from the questions and prodding that come from people outside the mainstream professional circle of educators. However, such diversity leads also to discomfort and conflict. Learning how to live with and grow through such discomfort is a significant challenge not just for schools but for every institution in our society.

In recent years researchers have challenged the notion that schools are culture-neutral and point out how schools are "dominated by the attitudes, beliefs, and value systems of one race and class of people" to the detriment of people from minority groups (Pine & Hillyard, 1990, p. 595). Studies have been conducted into the experience of students who come to schools from cultural, religious, or socioeconomic worlds different from the dominant school culture (Phelan, Davidson, & Yu, 1993; Rosaldo, 1989). These studies show that

> Schools have emphasized what working-class minority children lack in terms of the forms of language and knowledge sanctioned by the schools. This emphasis on so-called disadvantages has provided justification for lowered academic expectations and inaccurate portrayals of these children and their families. (Gonzalez et al., 1993, pp. 1–2)

But there are little data about how adults in the school influence and are influenced by the interaction between their home and professional cultures.

As one would expect, the data from Partners suggest that alignment of these cultures and belief systems contributed to a sense of belonging and efficacy in work.

> Because my mother is a teacher, and I have had lots of contact with teachers, I came in with a respect for them and an understanding of how difficult the job is. I didn't come in thinking the problem in education was the teachers, which was important in my being able to work with them. (BJ, 1/23/98)

In contrast, lack of alignment with the adult school culture was experienced by some Partners as a challenge to their belonging.

> I looked like the kids, had the same background as the kids. People don't think you deserve to be there, so I had to work doubly hard to be able to speak to be heard. The experience of the students is not valued, so my experience wasn't valued either. (GL, 1/23/98)

Unlike other challenges in the work of change facilitation that could be tackled with some professional objectivity, this one hit many Partners in the gut: They could not listen to the "deficit model" language so commonly used by teachers and administrators without feeling personally put down.

Just as students choose different strategies for negotiating between their multiple worlds (Phelan et al., 1993), so too did Partners. Some found it easier to sublimate aspects of their personal backgrounds; others struggled to reconcile their backgrounds with their school's culture. Some found it too difficult and chose to leave.

In a few cases, Partners turned the personal cost of change facilitation into an asset for the school. After months of questioning whether to continue for a 2nd year or leave, one Partner negotiated with the school and the organization to build a project more closely aligned to her personal interests: engaging parents in meaningful and respected ways in the school. "The difficulties in my first few months here with not feeling valued motivated me to stay because I realized that the school needed me. It needed a Latina on staff with 80 percent Latino children" (GL, 1/23/98). The conflict emerging from the lack of alignment between the background of the Partner and the dominant school culture influenced the direction of reform.

Varying Opinions About What Works

The third and related challenge comes from the varying perspectives on effective strategies for change. The mission of Partners in School Innovation is to increase achievement for low-income children in public schools through working in partnership with schools on whole-school change. When Partners understood and believed in the strategy of whole-school change, they felt a sense of security that they were in the right position for their own development and contribution.

> The more holistic, whole-school change approach is in line with my philosophy of how change can be effective in the long run. If we are going to have impact in society things need to change in a holistic way. So, for me, even though sometimes being a Partner was hard, I felt I was in the right place. (RM, 3/24/98)

Bringing into this work people who had experience in other strategies for social change, such as direct service and community organizing, meant that the strategy of whole-school change was frequently challenged. Whole-school change as a vehicle for broader social change raised tensions and concerns for those engaged in its messy implementation in actual schools. Its long-term timeline, its perceived trade-offs between focus on adult change and focus on student needs, its emphasis on structural changes without clear links to student outcomes—these are just a few of the problems.

The long-term nature of whole-school change sometimes conflicted with the sense of urgency about the need for change that the young people recruited into Partners had.

> I came in thinking that schools in the forefront of reform would have some urgency and do whatever it took to change. It was hard to realize even those who were committed to improve were also thinking about what was wrong with the students, or what the district wanted. For me the work never ends . . . it is life work. Others have the choice not to think about it: "I can just go home or go to another school." (GL, 1/23/98)

Personal learning and change often came through tension and conflict. While at first one might think it best to maximize the numbers of Partners whose personal backgrounds, interests, and experience are closely aligned with a school culture and change strategies, in fact, we have found much value also from working through the conflict that emerges from diversity of backgrounds and perspectives among our group members.

> The conflict and challenges . . . in particular around the issues of racism, was torturous. It pushed me to think a lot about my beliefs of efficacy and impact, and the role of Partners in society. It was painful, but I learned a lot. My brain was working hard in those conversations. (CJ, 1/18/98)

Questions

Further study is needed about how differences in background influence the efficacy and learning of adults in schools—change facilitators, teachers, and others—and about the institutional implications of such arrangements. How do personal backgrounds and belief systems shape the processes, goals, and outcomes of reform? What are the conditions within a school environment that support change facilitators from backgrounds different from those reflected in the dominant school culture?

We have learned that some important conditions in a school include: (1) tolerance of and skill in handling conflict; (2) active, public, and continual honoring of and respect for ethnic, cultural, and language diversity; (3) a diversity of people in positions of power in the school; and (4) explicit recognition on the part of school leaders of the existence of a dominant school culture along with efforts to make it more inclusive.

Given that all these conditions are rarely if ever met in one school at one time, we have also learned that it is important to deal with the limitations and struggles openly in the professional development of the Partners. Creating open, safe space to talk about the structural and cultural constraints imposed on some Partners—or students, or other change facilitators—and not on others is a continuing challenge. So is working out how to help such change facilitators negotiate the constraints in their own ways.

CONCLUSION

The experience of Partners in School Innovation suggests that a broad range of people can provide significant value to schools and to the individual and collective learning of teachers. In order for schools—especially those serving low-income and minority children—to meet the changing and increasing challenges that they face in contemporary society, teachers will need such ongoing support for their learning and growth. They cannot do it alone. Given appropriate training and support, outsiders without educational expertise can become valued inside supports to reformers within schools. However, neither this, nor any other route to change facilitation, is a panacea for school reform. More needs to be understood through research and practice about who can facilitate successful and lasting school change and how.

REFERENCES

Clandinin, D. J., & Connolly, F. M. (1995). *Teachers' professional knowledge landscapes*. New York: Teachers College Press.

Cochran-Smith, M., & Lytle, S. L. (Eds.). (1993). *Inside-Outside: Teacher research and knowledge*. New York: Teachers College Press.

Delpit, L. (1988). The silenced dialogue: Power and pedagogy in educating other people's children. *Harvard Educational Review, 58*(3), 280–298.

Freire, P. (1970). *Pedagogy of the oppressed*. (M. B. Ramos, Trans.). New York: Continuum.

Fullan, M. (1993). *Change forces: Probing the depths of education reform*. New York: Falmer Press.

Gonzalez, N., Moll, L., Floyd-Tenery, M., Rivera, A., Rendon, P., Gonzales, R., & Amanti, C. (1993). *Teacher research on funds of knowledge: Learning from households* (Report for National Center for Research on Cultural Diversity and Second Language Learning). Santa Cruz: University of California, Santa Cruz.

Hall, G., & Hord, S. (1987). *Change in schools: Facilitating the process*. Albany: State University of New York Press.

Hargreaves, A. (1996). Revisiting voice. *Educational Researcher, 25*(1), 12–19.

Lee, G., & Barnett, B. (1994). Using reflective questioning to promote collaborative dialogue. *Journal of Staff Development, 15*(1), 16–21.

Lieberman, A. (1995). Practices that support teacher development: Transforming conceptions of professional learning. *Phi Delta Kappan, 76*(8), 591–596.

Lieberman, A., Saxl, E., & Miles, M. (1988). Teacher leadership: Ideology and practice. In A. Lieberman (Ed.), *Building a professional culture in schools* (pp. 148–166). New York: Teachers College Press.

Loucks-Horsely, S., & Stiegelbauer, S. (1991). Using knowledge of change to guide staff development. In A. Lieberman & L. Miller (Eds.), *Staff development for education in the '90s* (pp. 15–36). New York: Teachers College Press.

McDonald, J. (1989). When outsiders try to change schools from the inside. *Phi Delta Kappan, 71*(3), 206–211.

McLaughlin, M. (1991). Enabling professional development: What have we learned? In A. Lieberman & L. Miller (Eds.), *Staff development for education in the '90s* (pp. 61–82). New York: Teachers College Press.

McLaughlin, M., & Yee, S. M. (1988). School as a place to have a career. In A. Lieberman (Ed.), *Building a professional culture in schools* (pp. 23–44). New York: Teachers College Press.

Meier, D. (1995). *The power of their ideas.* Boston: Beacon Press.

Miller, L. (1988). Unlikely beginnings: The district office as a starting point for developing a professional culture for teaching. In A. Lieberman (Ed.), *Building a professional culture in schools* (pp. 170–184). New York: Teachers College Press.

Moll, L., & Greenberg, J. (1990). Creating zones of possibilities: Combining social contexts for instruction. In L. Moll (Ed.), *Vygotsky and education* (pp. 319–348). New York: Cambridge University Press.

Nieto, S. (1996). *Affirming diversity.* White Plains, NY: Longman.

Palinscar, A. S., & Brown, A. L. (1984). Reciprocal teaching of comprehension-fostering and monitoring activities. *Cognition and Instruction, 1*(2), 117–175.

Phelan, P., Davidson, A. L., & Yu, H. C. (1993). Students' multiple worlds: Navigating the borders of family, peer and school cultures. In P. Phelan & A. L. Davidson (Eds.), *Renegotiating cultural diversity in American schools* (pp. 53–85). New York: Teachers College Press.

Pine, G., & Hilliard, A. (1990). Rx for racism: Imperative for America's schools. *Phi Delta Kappan, 71*(8), 593–600.

Putnam, R. T., & Borko, H. (2000). What do new views of knowledge and thinking have to say about research on teacher learning? *Educational Researcher, 29*(1), 4–15.

Rosaldo, R. (1989). *Culture and truth: The remaking of social analysis.* Boston: Beacon Press.

Sparks, D., & Hirsch, S. (1997). *New visions for staff development.* Alexandria, VA: Association for Supervision and Curriculum Development.

Chapter 5

Becoming a Teacher of Teachers: Two Dilemmas in Taking Up Preservice Supervision

Jon Snyder and Marianne D'Emidio-Caston

Numerous scholars and prestigious commissions (Carnegie Forum, 1986; Holmes Group, 1986; National Commission, 1997) argue that the current wave of educational reform must be sustained by an aggressive, focused reinvention of the way new teachers are educated and socialized into the profession (Darling-Hammond, 1995; Lieberman & Miller, 1991). Exceptionally qualified teachers require exceptional teacher education guided by qualified teacher educators who are capable of helping candidates use theory and practice and make the transition from student to professional educator. Surprisingly, little has been reported regarding either the learning and development of teacher educators or how individuals grow into this role. If teacher education is to become a critical instrument in the reshaping of the teaching profession, then rigorous inquiry is needed into the distinctive demands of the teacher educator role as well as the conditions that support and constrain development toward meeting those demands. In this chapter, we describe two novice teacher educators working in the role of supervisor in preservice teacher education. We focus on how their perspectives about the teaching of teachers shift as they learn to negotiate two essential dilemmas of the preservice supervisor's role: (1) bridging research and teaching, and (2) balancing supervision and mentoring.

BACKGROUND

Two antithetical conceptualizations of teacher education, and thus of supervision, dominate the field (Darling-Hammond with Sclan, 1992; Sergiovanni & Starratt, 1998).

> These conceptions vary primarily in the extent to which they view learning as either predictable and standardized or differentiated and complex—and teaching as the mastery of simple routines or as the exercise of informed judgment. (Darling-Hammond with Sclan, 1992, p. 15)

Where teaching is viewed as mastery of routine, teachers, according to Darling-Hammond (1995), are seen as "implementors of external-ly designed and prescribed curriculum" (p. 21), and the consequent function of teacher preparation is viewed as the transfer of the right set of prescriptions and procedures standardized enough to be listed and checked by evaluators during short visits to classrooms (Darling-Hammond with Sclan, 1992). This older model of teacher education derives from Taylor's scientific management theory. It employs bureau-cratic organizational structures to promote and regulate the transfer of a body of knowledge often referred to as the "canon" or the "basics." Informed by theories of management, such as MacGregor's Theory X, which envision teachers as factory workers, traditional visions of teacher education expect teachers to comply with the demands of those in higher positions of authority. Motivated by rewards and punish-ments, teachers, from this perspective, should develop certain traits, in-structional skills, and specific behaviors; and supervisors are under-stood as the experts who know these traits and are granted the authority to monitor teachers' adherence to them (e.g., Hunter, 1984; Minton, 1979). In this tradition of teacher education, learning how to teach is learning a set of skills and the rules for when to use them.

Where teaching is envisioned as the exercise of informed judgment, the "function of teacher preparation [is seen] as empowering teachers to own, use, and develop knowledge about teaching and learning" (Darling-Hammond, 1995, p. 22). Sergiovanni and Starratt (1998) de-scribe this second framing of teacher education as rooted in the profes-sional and moral authority of self-governing and self-managing teach-ers, who in turn make the traditional conceptions of supervision obsolete. Such a professional vision contrasts sharply with a deeply in-grained and widely accepted view of teachers as technicians. This newer vision of teacher preparation responds to a more inclusive view of society and educational purpose. This is a vision that emphasizes community as a source of support for identity building and moral agency. In this framework, supervision derives from theories of management, such as MacGregor's Theory Y, that assume an inherent, active capacity of both teacher and learner to take responsibility for learning. This model can be described as "learning from teaching." In this tradition, the supervisory function is to organize resources and manage organizational conditions so members of the learning community "can best achieve their own goals by directing their own efforts toward organizational objectives" (Sergiovanni & Starratt, 1998, p. 16).

Schön (1983, 1987) describes how professionals generate knowledge as they engage in their work, forming intuitions about what is called for in a given situation. Individuals form these intuitions (hunches) through their experience of success and failure in their past practice. Given this understanding, the role of supervisor is to help the practitioner engage in reflective practice that illuminates the "'tacit knowledge' that was operative in the teaching episode" (Sergiovanni & Starratt, 1998, p. 129). Tracy and MacNaughton (1993) use the term "teacher concern" model to describe supervisory practice that facilitates and assists the teacher. They contrast this with practices that place emphasis on the evaluative supervisory role found in the "learning how to teach" model. With greater awareness of their practice, teachers move toward more informed judgment in their work with learners.

THE STUDY

This study documents the first 18 months of the work of two beginning supervisors of preservice teachers in the elementary teacher education program at the University of California at Santa Barbara (UCSB). We interviewed both supervisors and observed them at work with student teachers in the schools and in meetings at the university. Over the period of the study both readily shared with us their notes and observations about their work with the student teachers. Drawing on this material, we have developed two case studies that provide insight into becoming a teacher of teachers. We focus particularly on the professional strengths that the two supervisors felt they brought with them to the role, their concerns and issues as they learned the role, and the supports each believe might have helped them as they took up their work with preservice teacher candidates.

THE SETTING

UCSB offers an intensive 13-month (an academic year sandwiched by two summers) combined credential and master's in education program.

Over the past 4 years the program revised the following program essentials:

- *Standards for candidates.* Teacher candidates are now required to meet the California Standards for the Teaching Profession.
- *Curriculum.* The curriculum has been reconceived and reorganized to make explicit the differentiation and integration of knowledge of content, children, and pedagogy to enhance access to opportunities for learning for all children.
- *Assessment process.* Multiple-function portfolios, case studies of learners, and videotapes have either been introduced or revised.
- *Relations with schools or districts and school-based educators.* We are now clustering resources and relationships in seven partnership schools. (See Snyder, 1996, for a more complete description.)

These changes constitute a conscious shift from a learning how to teach model to a learning from teaching model. While much has been written of changes in UCSB's teacher education program (Copeland, Birmingham, DeMeulle, Natal, & D'Emidio-Caston, 1994; Copeland & D'Emidio-Caston, 1997; Heras, 1996; Heras & Floriani, 1997; Snyder, Lewin, & Lippincott, 1996; Snyder, Lippincott, & Bower, 1998), this is the first research study in this context to document and analyze becoming a teacher of teachers in a supervisory role.

In teacher education programs where fully supported institutional faculty do not perform this function (still the majority of programs), two career paths generate the personnel who become supervisors. The first route is often followed by experienced classroom teachers who choose to return to graduate school with the intent of becoming career teacher educators. For many of these graduate students/teachers, becoming a supervisor of preservice students provides financial support for graduate studies as well as an internship in teacher education. The second route is followed by classroom teachers who, nearing the end of their careers, choose to "give something back" to the profession. Many of these retiring teachers anticipate deriving professional satisfaction and personal enjoyment from the work.

THE NEW SUPERVISORS

The two supervisors we follow fit the two general paths into supervision outlined above. Both began as supervisors in the same semester. At the time of this writing, both had been members of the teacher education supervision team for 2 years. Carolyn taught elementary school in a neighboring state for several decades before relocating to earn a doctorate. Susan is a retired teacher with 27 years of classroom practice in one local school where she also served as a cooperating teacher for students in the UCSB program. Perhaps, the most insightful description of the two supervisors is encapsulated in the words they used to introduce themselves to the teacher candidates. Carolyn's first words were "I am an ethnographer." In contrast, Susan began with "I am a teacher with 27 years of experience working at K. School."

Biography and the ways in which one sees life clearly have a role in determining how new supervisors take up their role (Sergiovanni & Starratt, 1998). We cannot ignore this. Hence we try to let our colleagues speak for themselves about their experience and about their understandings and concerns about their work as supervisors and the process of teacher education at UCSB.

Carolyn

Carolyn saw her own career as a movement from teacher to researcher: "I was a classroom teacher and became an ethnographer." At the same time, she retained a skeptical practitioner's point of view regarding the value of research, noting "a great huge gulf between research and practice." She reiterated the oft-heard lament of teachers disconnected from the literature of their profession:

> A lot of the experimental research looking at classrooms and reading and writing in classrooms that way, where they either pull somebody out and put them in a laboratory and test them or take quick looks, . . . as teachers we knew that they weren't getting the real picture.

Carolyn felt she had much of value to offer student teachers in terms of "bridging" research and practice.

> I came from not just theory, which is getting my doctorate at UCSB, but with a lot of experience. I still think that's one of my strengths. It is not just my practical experience and not just my

work in getting my doctorate but the combination of the two and kind of a blending of the two in that I feel like I can make a bridge between research and practice. I thought I had a lot to offer them, not only how to interpret the theory they were getting from the university as I watched them in the classrooms but also more practical things about how I could help them become student teachers in the classroom.

Carolyn's familiarity with research emerged often. For instance, at the beginning of her 2nd year in the role, she participated with other supervisors in designing a workshop and format for lesson planning. She contributed three references she found in the ERIC database to inform the work of the group. Another instance of the strength Carolyn describes as bridging research and practice, came in midfall of her 2nd year at a workshop designed for cooperating teachers and UCSB faculty on California's recent *Reading Initiative*. In a discussion of the state document emphasizing a skills-based, phonics-driven approach to reading instruction, Carolyn used her understanding of different types of research to critique the research used to support the document's assumptions about learning to read. Without the knowledge she shared, the workshop participants would have left with a different and less sophisticated understanding of the document. A third instance of Carolyn's linking ethnographic research techniques to practice as a support for student teachers came early in the winter quarter of her 2nd year. At this time, student teachers begin a second placement in a new classroom months after the classroom culture is established. Carolyn offered two workshops on using ethnographic techniques (note taking, note making, ethnographic interviews) to gain access to a preexisting culture.

These examples of Carolyn's use of her research skills in teacher education highlight a difference between *research* as a set of practices (e.g., a library literature review, a set of data-gathering techniques) and *theory* as a set of abstractions to shape one's thoughts, attitudes, and actions within the world.

Balancing Research and Teaching. Despite her successes, Carolyn found that bridging the gulf between research and teaching—with teacher candidates, school- and college-based educators, and even within herself—proved more challenging than she originally anticipated. She commented,

This is my 2nd year of supervision and now I have a million more questions and I am a lot less comfortable that what I'm doing is the right way to do it. . . . It is almost as if I have the background and I have the desire and I have great students and I have great placements and great everything I could possibly need, and yet it is still not working for me.

Nearing the end of her 2nd year as supervisor, however, Carolyn saw supervision and ethnography in a difficult tension that she felt unable to resolve.

One of the reasons I think you valued me when I first started working were my ethnographic skills of observation, and I'm finding more and more that it doesn't help me as much as I thought it would help me. It helps me when I go in a classroom. It helps me to observe the richness of it and the details of it, but as a supervisor I am doing exactly what I would not do as an ethnographer which is to step in for an hour once or twice a week. . . .

I found myself getting into trouble a lot of times because as a supervisor you have to evaluate and make judgments, which is another thing I wouldn't do if I were an ethnographer, and that is something I am coming to understand a supervisor must do.

Balancing Mentor and Supervisor Roles. Carolyn perceived herself as having an ability to work with people. The multiple and varied social relationships inherent in supervising student teachers, however, surprised her. She stated with a laugh, "This job has been a lot easier this year once I accepted the idea that you have to work at these personal relationships." Her understanding of the particular and different types of relationships grew over time.

Along with all the content and all the subject matter that a supervisor has to know and the experience and the theory and the talking to the kids and lesson plans and classroom management . . . along with all that . . . is this rapport that you need to have with these kids who are becoming teachers. You also have to have this personal relationship with the principal. You also have to have it with the cooperating teacher and you have to have it with the Teacher Ed supervisors and the instructors so there's tons of different people that a supervisor has to be the liaison between . . . and that's really . . . very exhausting because you have to go from one social situation where you have a particular role to another one where your role is entirely different.

Related to her sense of disjuncture between ethnography and supervision, Carolyn, like many new supervisors, experienced a relational tension in balancing her two institutional functions of mentoring and supervision. In broad strokes, supervision involves using one's positional and experiential authority to evaluate performance. At very basic levels, a supervisor is indeed "above" one's supervisees, is responsible for evaluating one's supervisees, and in fairness should "tell" one's supervisees what the expectations are. A mentor, on the other hand, has neither the positional authority nor the institutional responsibility for evaluation. A mentor listens and observes, seeks to understand and support, and, even if possessing experiential authority, maintains a basic human equality with one's mentees. Those who work with beginning professionals find themselves needing to fulfill both functions simultaneously—a difficult challenge for anyone, including Carolyn.

> I work very hard, at least I try to show them that we (the student teacher and the supervisor) are on the same level, that they can come to me as a friend and a person and I can talk to them about it. That gets me into trouble a lot of times. . . . [Last year] I wasn't strong enough to say to [a student teacher], "You're full of baloney." But at the same time it is helpful. If they see this [hand gesture indicating hierarchy] they aren't going to tell me, . . . a lot of things that [another student teacher] has told me, she never would have told me, if we didn't have this kind of back and forth relationship.

On the one hand, Carolyn wanted to be the equal of her student teachers, but she did know more than they. She wanted to be nonjudgmental, but she was a key actor in high-stakes decisions. On the other hand, she knew from her experience as a teacher and a classroom ethnographer that telling does not constitute teaching, let alone learning.

> You have all this knowledge and you want to start giving these kids all this stuff that they don't have. In that first year I'd see things as an experienced teacher I could help them with and so I did sometimes and that didn't help them a bit because they weren't able to think it out themselves. It is not my job to walk them through, because the minute I start walking them through things then I've taken over for them and I'm telling them you can't do this on your own.

By the middle of the 2nd year, however, Carolyn had developed a balance between her authority and her humanity. "I'm coming to accept that I do know more, and I have to figure out ways of working with them so that they construct the knowledge." Two cooperating teachers expressed concerns that student teachers placed in their classrooms were not spending enough time in the classroom. Carolyn explains, "The problems were very minor . . . they leave their class to run off dittos for their university assignments." In another instance, "I found a student teacher in the teachers' lounge . . . making phone calls during PE time."

Carolyn found that balancing her supervisor and mentor roles with cooperating teachers was almost as difficult as finding the balance with student teachers. With clusters of students at each partnership school, more cooperating teachers participate in the process of teacher education. Increasing the number of school-based educators directly involved in teacher education creates new opportunities for relationships but requires more time and energy on the part of the supervisor. "I didn't realize," Carolyn laments,

> how much teaching of cooperating teachers I had to do. I've been
> working all year with cooperating teachers telling them the most
> important thing is that communication right at the beginning. It is
> like they didn't hear that or I have to give them ways of how to
> communicate with their beginning teacher and I have to give them
> ways to accept this new teacher into their classroom.

Carolyn knew it would be simple to talk with the student teachers about the cooperating teachers' concerns. She also knew it would violate her principle of equal relationship as well as interrupt the communication of the cooperating teachers with the student teachers. Carolyn solved her dilemma by "devising ways of getting the cooperating teachers to speak directly to the student teachers about this issue." She did not tell either the student teachers or the cooperating teachers what to do. Rather, she told both parties that they needed to have a meeting. By "not telling anyone the answer," Carolyn exhibited an understanding that her roles included "teaching these two very valuable cooperating teachers how to talk with student teachers." In doing so, she balanced her mentor and supervisory roles with the student teachers, as well as met the supervisory relationship expected by the cooperating teachers. She balanced raising the student teachers' awareness of classroom responsibilities and increasing the cooperating teachers' expertise as teacher educators.

If I had taken it on and said, "You naughty preservice kids, you're not doing this right," then I would have gone to this level (holds one hand higher than the other). I would have also stopped the ability of these four people to communicate together, which is ultimately more important. So I could have fixed the little situation but it would not really work in the bigger situation. I figured it out. I'm starting to think like a supervisor.

What Would Have Helped. Carolyn believes that an internship in supervision would have helped her navigate the challenges of the role in a way that would have better supported the candidates with whom she worked.

If I could have seen what it looked like and understood a little more . . . to actually follow two experienced supervisors around it would have helped me through the 3 years that it takes you to become a supervisor. I wish I was paid as a supervisor for the first placement and I could just, not supervise, but I could just hold on to experienced supervisors or just be attached to them while they go about their job.

Carolyn also suggested that a reading list and opportunities to discuss literature on supervision might have helped her as well. "I didn't read anything about it, I mean, I learn a lot by reading."

Susan

Susan felt she brought two strengths with her as a beginning supervisor. First, she brought a professional passion for the role. "I bring," she stated, "the joy and the love of teaching. I always, always, always supported the student teaching program because I just feel it is such an important part of the future of education." She named her second perceived strength as context-specific knowledge of the teacher education program and of local schools. As a retired teacher familiar with the schools and teachers in the area, Susan understood both UCSB's program philosophy and the way local schools work. Speaking of herself, she says,

You kind of know the way a school works and you know that when the bell rings everybody's in their room no matter what. . . . Sometimes during recess you think you are so important that you need to get your little comment made to the teacher. Maybe they need to call a parent and that's much more important than what you need to say at that moment so you better figure out another way to communicate with them.

She also had personal and professional relationships with the teachers in the schools. "I got to work in an environment where I was already a familiar person, so that when I was at E. School, I knew enough people that I felt comfortable right away." Finally, she knew the assignments given by UCSB instructors because she had worked with many student teachers in her own classroom prior to becoming a supervisor.

I have seen those lessons given a lot. I know what the instructor is getting at. So that helps me with the student teachers, that helps me with the cooperating teachers. I think I brought lots of experience, I think I brought a good command of what a cooperating teacher's role is. I think I brought stories and anecdotes that I can share with the teachers so that when they talk about something I can say [to them as a way of showing that "I've been there"], "Oh, yeah, that has happened a hundred times. You are not the first person who has ever had that happen."

Balancing Research and Teaching. Like Carolyn, Susan used the metaphor of a bridge to explain the role, but she was bridging between people and places rather than between research and teaching. "I see it as the bridge. . . . I either start at the university and go backwards to the school or I start at the school and go forward to the university. Or I go both ways." Susan sees the supervisor's role as linking the school and the university—the university instructor and the cooperating teacher—through her skills of negotiation.

When the cooperating teachers come to me and say, "Gosh this seems like a really difficult assignment. Can you help me clear this up?" I have to take a step back and say, "You know what, I have to get more information about this before I can help clear this up for you. Talk to your student teacher. Find out if they can give you any more insight than what they have already given you. In the mean time I'll talk to the instructor."

Susan also sees the supervisor's role as linking within the university so she is bridging both between and within institutions. "I'm like the facilitator for everybody."

Unlike Carolyn, Susan did not feel she had academic research expertise. "I don't come from a research background and so oftentimes when there is talk about research-based this or that, I am not as familiar with that side of it." On the other hand, she did bring a history of rigorous inquiry into teaching. "I do in a way come from a research base because of having been a teacher for so many years, I mean, that is my research. But it is not anything that I can open a book and say, 'Well, according to so and so . . . ' It is based on just my experience." Susan's experiential theoretical frame, those conceptions of teaching and learning that guided her thinking about her experience, was consistent with the central ideas of the UCSB teacher education program.

> I think you really need to understand the philosophy of the university that you are working with and make sure that what you have always felt about education lines up with that close enough that you can really support the university. So that you are not constantly saying, "Well, OK, that is what they are telling you, but in my experience as an educator this is what I know to be true."

Susan's guidance to student teachers came from a single source—her experience. She did not experience Carolyn's cognitive challenge of bridging her experience as a teacher, her experience as a researcher, and her emerging experience as a teacher educator.

> My student teachers were really asking me about classroom management. . . . They are really starting to question checks on the board, stars, points, and coupons and having an auction and blah, blah, blah. . . . "How did [you] do classroom management? Is classroom management doable without having all of that stuff?" . . . I told them what I thought and how I did it and this that and the next thing, but then I had to end my whole story with . . . "That was just the way I do it. That isn't necessarily the way to do it. That is the way I did it and it felt right for me and it was authentic for me and it worked for me because it came from me. It wasn't that I read that in a book." . . . Maybe I would have rather said to them, "You can go read this and this and this and then you can take the whole thing and then put it together and make meaning for yourself." On the other hand, I do not feel like I don't have answers. I feel like I have answers to help them, but it's not just directing them to articles and things like that.

Balancing Mentor and Supervisor Roles. While a little shocked at the time demands, Susan understood the relational aspects of the supervisory role.

> You have to be a really flexible person so that you can work with colleagues, your own colleagues, work with the cooperating teachers, work with administrators in schools, work with the students, be they 21-year-old recent graduates or 45-year-old people that have been out in the business world.

On one hand, she retained a discomfort with the power differential associated with the term *supervision*: "I have a hard time with the word *supervisor*. Supervisor seems like you're the superior person and I don't really see the role as that. I see it more as a mentorship. It is not that I am the superior supervisor person." She characterizes her role much more along the lines of the mentor:

> I think there is a fine line between being their friend and being their supervisor. I see my role more as a mentorship helping them make sense of what their understanding is. . . . I feel like my function is to support the student teacher above everything else. I think it is just really important that the student teachers have a supervisor who values them, their work, and who they are, who sees them as a human being before a student teacher. Basically that is the way I feel about life.

On the other hand, she felt that the evaluative component of supervision was absolutely essential, and she took it up with seriousness, conceiving of herself as the "gatekeeper to the profession." She defines the caliber of the job a supervisor does in terms of knowing a student well enough to write a letter of recommendation. Speaking of her experience with supervisors as a cooperating teacher, she noted:

> It mattered who the person was who came. If they were very committed, if they had a deep understanding of the program, if they really worked with the university . . . that person had a much bigger impact on the student teacher than the supervisor who had 14 other things to do and was just doing this as one other little thing . . . maybe came three or four times in a whole semester. That really bothered me because I felt like that person was carrying a lot of weight in the writing up of a recommendation for that per-

son, and sometimes I didn't feel like the supervisor really had a very good feeling of who this person really was.

For Susan, mentoring and supervising were flip sides of the same coin, and the coin that contained both was a sustained and trusting relationship. The key element, according to Susan, to building and maintaining a relationship that could support mentoring and supervising is communication. "To be a really good communicator in terms of speaking and listening, you have to be able to read between the lines of what the student teachers are saying and not saying." This is an area where Susan felt she grew considerably in her first 2 years in the role.

Where Carolyn felt she did not do enough telling early in her supervisory work, Susan describes her first year as one where she might have done too much telling.

> I feel a lot more confident listening. I think last year I gave too many answers. This year I'm much better at listening and then the student teachers keep talking and then pretty soon they are working it out themselves or they are bringing up some really juicy questions. Then I say, "OK, those are good questions." I wait and listen and let them work it through. Rather than trying to second-guess what they are asking and providing them with the answers. I think that was definitely a weakness last year because I was kind of in the quick fix mode. . . . I feel more confident about seeing the importance of them working it out themselves. However, there are times when they ask me things that I know, I can just tell they need just the answer and so I just give it to them, but much more the other way this year than giving them the answer every time. If it is what I call a nuts-and-bolts question, I tend to give them an answer.

What Would Have Helped. Like Carolyn, Susan requested an internship in supervision. "Maybe having some relationship with a person who is a supervisor before you take on the role so that you would sort of see how it works. Some type of shadowing so that you would sort of see how that goes." Unlike Carolyn, Susan did not request a review of the supervisory literature, but she did request opportunities to become "more familiar with the resources that are available in the teacher education office." Most of these resources are what Carolyn called the "literature on supervision." Thus, both Susan and Carolyn requested a "student supervising" period comparable to a student teaching experience and ongoing opportunities to read about, and discuss with their colleagues, the research, theory, and practice of preservice supervision.

IMPLICATIONS

If teacher preparation premised on the "how to" model could meet our goals for student learning then preservice teacher supervisors would not face the challenges Carolyn and Susan faced. There would be incontrovertible right answers from research that supervisors could tell candidates to follow. The mentor role would be separate from the right answers and involve a shoulder upon which to cry and a few emotional coping mechanisms for the trauma of transition.

Learning from teaching, however, requires more. Teaching and learning, like life itself, are inherently ambiguous. Learning how to learn from teaching requires that supervisors mentor candidates through terrain that is inextricably and simultaneously both cognitively and emotionally challenging. Thus supervision of teachers and teacher candidates is neither telling as in one tradition of supervision nor mentoring from a psychotherapeutic tradition. It is some of each but neither. Supervision is the teaching of teachers. Teaching teachers requires traditional supervisory knowledge, skills, and dispositions. Teaching teachers involves helping teacher candidates develop productive ways of understanding and working with children, content knowledge, and pedagogy. Often the teacher of teachers will know some things that teacher candidates do not yet know and will have to take responsibility for helping teacher candidates learn those more productive understandings and actions that support student learning and development. Often the teacher of teachers will have to take a stand and point out the difference between what is appropriate and what is not.

There are facets of teacher preparation that require of supervisors the knowledge, skills, and dispositions traditionally associated with mentoring. Teaching teachers involves helping candidates balance the emotional challenges of passion and compassion and of dizzying wins and crushing defeats. The teacher of teachers must know about and be adept in interpersonal communication skills. He or she must have empathy and, without prying or assuming a therapist's role, must be able to facilitate a constructive flow between the cognitive and the affective. Like all teachers, teachers of teachers must know their students. And, teachers of teachers must always maintain a basic human equality with and respect for their students.

Little wonder then that these two teachers of teachers both grappled with bridging the worlds of research and teaching and balancing the roles of mentoring and supervising. Because they entered from different career paths and with different personalities, Susan's and Carolyn's struggles with the role of student teacher supervisor were as different as their career trajectories. While Susan will continue as a supervisor with the teacher education program, Carolyn is leaving UCSB to take a tenure-track position at another institution. Her move highlights one of the major challenges of the graduate student model: By the time the intern-supervisor learns the role, she or he leaves the position.

The nature of Susan's and Carolyn's growth over their first 2 years in the role and the fact that they proposed nearly identical suggestions for professional support provide some important lessons for the field:

• Initial performance and an ongoing sense of efficacy seem to be enhanced when supervisors of student teachers know, understand, and believe in the values and conceptions of teaching and learning that undergird the program in which they are working. This highlights the importance of hiring criteria and processes that are congruent with those of the teacher education program.

• Before they take on full responsibilities of the role, supervisors could benefit from the same types of opportunities for learning that have been shown to be beneficial to teacher candidates:
  A common, clear vision of good teaching
  A structured internship carefully chosen to support the ideas and practices that undergird the program
  Well-defined standards of practice and performance that are used to guide practice and growth

• Ongoing support is crucial to supervisors' professional growth and should be provided in ways that build on and use the different yet complementary strengths of different individuals within the supervisor's cohort including:
  Opportunities to build strong relationships, common knowledge, and shared beliefs among school- and university-based educators
  Extensive use of case study methods, teacher research, performance assessments, and portfolio evaluations to ground candidate and supervisory learning in the data of practice

Studies like this highlight the importance and complexity of preservice teacher supervision in the preparation of teachers. While the implications of this study for selection, preparation, and ongoing support for preservice supervisors are clearer to us, we recognize that institutional policies in higher education often legislate against conditions that support the growth and development of preservice supervisors. The role, for instance, is rarely considered of equal importance with research or advising Ph.D. students in promotion and tenure decisions. Often the role is part-time, with those holding the job utilized as interchangeable parts rather than valued as essential actors in a well-integrated and critically important educational enterprise. If teacher education is to achieve the goal of preparing teachers who learn from teaching, who are capable of supporting the kinds of student learning required for academic and personal success, then further research must be conducted into the role of preservice supervisors and the conditions that support their growth. Furthermore, those institutions charged with the legal and ethical responsibility for the professional preparation of teachers must authenticate the role of supervisor as an essential and rewarded function of higher education.

REFERENCES

Bartell, C. (1995). Shaping teacher induction policy in California. *Teacher Education Quarterly*, *22*(4), 27–43.

Carnegie Forum on Education and the Economy. (1986). *A nation prepared: Teachers for the twenty-first century*. Washington, DC: Author.

Cogan, M. (1973). *Clinical supervision*. Boston: Houghton Mifflin.

Copeland, W. D., Birmingham, C., DeMuelle, L., Natal, D., & D'Emidio-Caston, M. (1994). Making meaning in classrooms: An investigation of cognitive processes in aspiring teachers, experienced teachers, and their peers. *American Educational Research Journal*, *31*(1), 166–196.

Copeland, W. D., & D'Emidio-Caston, M. (1997). Indicators of development of practical theory in pre-service teacher education students. *Teaching and Teacher Education*, *14*(5), 513–534.

Darling-Hammond, L. (1995). Changing the conceptions of teaching and teacher development. *Teacher Education Quarterly*, *22*(4), 9–26.

Darling-Hammond, L. (1997). *The right to learn*. San Francisco: Jossey-Bass.

Darling-Hammond, L. (with Sclan, E.). (1992). Policy and supervision. In C. D. Glickman (Ed.), *Supervision in transition* (pp. 7–29). Alexandria, VA: Association for Supervision and Curriculum Development.

Goldhammer, R. (1969). *Clinical supervision*. New York: Holt, Rinehart and Winston.

Heras, A. (1996). *Documentation of Year 1 of the ABRE project*. Unpublished report prepared for U.S. Department of Education.

Heras, A., & Floriani, A. (1997). *Follow-up study of UCSB graduates*. Unpublished report prepared for Graduate School of Education, University of California, Santa Barbara.

Holmes Group. (1986). *Tomorrow's teachers: A report of the Holmes Group*. East Lansing, MI: Author.

Hunter, M. (1984). Knowing, teaching, and supervising. In P. L. Hosford (Ed.), *Using what we know about teaching*, pp. 169–203. Alexandria, VA: Association for Supervision and Curriculum Development.

Lieberman, A., & Miller, L. (1991). *Staff development for education in the '90s.* New York: Teachers College Press.

Minton, E. (1979). *Clinical supervision: Developing evaluation skills for dynamic leadership* [cassette recording]. Englewood, CO: Educational Consulting Associates.

National Commission on Teaching and America's Future. (1997). *What matters most: Teaching for America's future.* New York: Author.

Oja, S. N. (1991). Adult development. In A. Lieberman & L. Miller (Eds.), *Staff development for education in the '90s* (pp. 37–60). New York: Teachers College Press.

Schön, D. (1983). *The reflective practitioner: How professionals think in action.* New York: Basic Books.

Schön, D. (1987). *Educating the reflective practitioner.* San Francisco: Jossey-Bass.

Sergiovanni, T., & Starratt, R. (1998). *Supervision: A redefinition.* New York: McGraw-Hill.

Snyder, J. (1996). *The University of California–Santa Barbara experimental teacher education program.* Report prepared for the California Commission on Teacher Credentialing, Sacramento, CA.

Snyder, J., Lewin, B., & Lippincott, A. C. (1996, April). *Learning organizations, leadership, and teacher education: A self study in three takes.* Paper presented at the annual meeting of the American Educational Research Association, New York.

Snyder, J., Lippincott, A. C., & Bower, D. (1998). Portfolios in teacher education: Technical or transformational? In Nona Lyons (Ed.), *With portfolio in hand: Portfolios in teaching and teacher education* (pp. 123–142). New York: Teachers College Press.

Tracy, S. J., & MacNaughton, R. H. (1993). *Assisting and assessing educational personnel.* Boston: Allyn and Bacon.

Chapter 6

Reform in the Intermediary Zone: Change Agent Among Change Agents

Cheryl J. Craig

Early in 1998 I became a planning and evaluation consultant to five local schools associated with a national reform initiative. This was a new and unusual role for me—a personal invitation that came on the heels of my appointment as a senior researcher and professor at a local university. Though I was curious about reformers and reform movements and about how their philosophies and practices might be similar to and different from mine, I had no direct experiences with either organized reform movements or with educators who consider themselves reformers. I was a western Canadian who had studied schooling and teachers in that context. I had taught for several years in public schools and also had years of experience as a curriculum consultant in a large urban district. In the latter role I worked closely with numerous schools and groups of educators, creating spaces for authentic discussions of curriculum, pedagogy, and emergent issues relating to student learning, but I was new to the particular U.S. city and to U.S. public education.

From my perspective it seemed that certain kinds of change initiatives create a sense of abrupt intervention, rather than dynamic emergence, on the professional knowledge landscapes of schools (Clandinin & Connelly, 1995). Thus I recognized that there was much to learn about the complex ways that whole-school reform shapes the horizons of educators' experiences. On the one hand, my role as planning

and evaluation consultant meant that I would assist school-based educators with articulating and enacting their plans and with developing
their in-school research records. On the other hand, I understood that
the same school-based educators would inform my understanding of
the influence of school reform on teachers' knowledge, communities
of knowing (Craig, 1995, 1998), and school contexts. Such mutually
beneficial arrangements emerge in what I will call in this chapter the
intermediary zone. To me, the intermediary zone is a distinct middle
ground where people situated in different places in the educational enterprise meet to productively address topics, issues, and challenges of
mutual concern in the field of education, a place where relationships
are collaborative, inquiry based, and action oriented. In the intermediary zone, as I hope this narrative will show, various dilemmas that
accompany the process of change are addressed—most obvious among
these being the place and role of change agents.

DEFINING SPACES AND DETERMINING ROLES

The reform initiative sought to nurture teacher learning, to personalize
the learning environment, and to break down isolation between and
among students, teachers, schools, and communities. Its overall purpose
was to improve the quality of learning for more urban youth. Thus,
as the principals and I began to negotiate our various roles, it seemed
appropriate to find ways to describe and share with one another the
various settings in which we worked and the various expectations that
each of us held for the reform initiative in those settings.

The Principals' Position

The first planning group meeting of the five principals and me began
with a discussion of a popular Thomas Jefferson quotation that fit the
occasion:

> I know of no safe depository of the ultimate powers of the society but the
> people themselves; and if we think them not enlightened enough to exer-
> cise their control with a wholesome discretion, the remedy is not to take it
> from them, but to inform their discretion by education. (Letter to William
> C. Jarvis, Sept. 28, 1820)

Jefferson's words opened up spaces for a lively conversation regarding
who the principals and I were in the work, and how we saw ourselves

and others located in relation to the reform movement and each other. The principals spoke of having faith in the individual school efforts. They expressed admiration for the other educators involved and for their schools. They wondered what local participation in a national reform movement might mean. As one might predict, they did not want their schools written up in a less-than-positive manner; they did not want test scores to be the sole determinants of success and failure.

The principals' concern for broad and comprehensive portraits of their schools led them to invite me to work as an intermediary who would understand the positions they held and help them and their faculties find satisfying ways to interact with the reform movement's agenda. They also wanted assistance in capturing how and in what ways the reform agenda might be taking hold in their schools. They desired an approach for dissemination that would have some degree of transferability (Lincoln & Guba, 1989; Mishler, 1990) to other individuals and schools about to engage in whole-school change.

The School Partners

The urban schools with which I worked as an intermediary represented a rich cross section of American society. While all of the schools sought to be racially balanced, they tended also to represent the different parts of the city and districts in which they were situated. With the use of pseudonyms, the schools will now be introduced.

Martha Maude Cochrane Academy—elementary school; 545 predominantly African American students; Metropolitan Area School District #1

Hardy Academy—middle school; 500 predominantly African American students; Metropolitan Area School District #1

Eagle High School—2,300 predominantly African American and Spanish-speaking students; Metropolitan Area School District #1.

Heights Community Learning Center—elementary school; 365 predominantly Spanish-speaking immigrant students; Metropolitan Area School District #2.

T. P. Yaeger Middle School—1,500 students, of which roughly one third were White or Asian American, one third African American, and one third Mexican American and Mexican immigrants; Metropolitan Area School District #2.

Each school had a "story of school" (Clandinin & Connelly, 1996), a social narrative history that had made it eligible for funding and support from the reform initiative, a social narrative history that in some ways each school was expected to continue to live into. Each also had a "story of reform" (Craig, 2001) that had been formed—that is, narrated—by school-based change agents around the imperatives of the reform initiative, particularly improving student learning. Hardy Academy and T. P. Yaeger Middle School provide a good illustration of this point.

Hardy Academy. When I began my work with Hardy Academy, its reform team had disbanded. None of the faculty members who had signed the original grant application remained at the school. Some had transferred to new positions when the previous principal was appointed to a larger school in another district; others had simply retired. After many telephone inquiries, I was able to contact one teacher. Miraculously, she was able to pull together a new team whose strength and collegiality with one another and with me were so convincing that both the school district representatives and the incoming principal were of the opinion that the group was the original one, minus the principal who had left. At the time, no one wanted to spoil the compliment by breathing a word to the contrary.

T. P. Yaeger Middle School. Where T. P. Yaeger Middle School was concerned, the leadership had elected to hold onto the reform until the local reform network office was established. In the meantime, the principal retired, causing many to wonder whether the reform endeavor would become extinguished in a leadership change. In the transition phase, a strong team of 18 school-based educators came together. Over the next months, the team invited the full faculty to make decisions about the reform plan and the budget—decisions that had previously been determined in other ways. Later, when an on-site administrator was appointed principal, the entire faculty was invited to participate in developing the budget. When a meeting was called in the 1999–2000 academic year to discuss how to present evidence concerning the school's reform effort, 45 of Yaeger's 85 faculty members attended of their own accord; some came conveying the support of additional teacher colleagues.

My Role in Planning and Evaluation

Not long after I agreed to work with the five school faculties in 1998, but shortly before the role of planning and evaluation consultants was formally defined by the local reform committee, the principals and I developed an outline to guide my participation. Officially, I was an employee of the university with research, teaching, and service responsibilities. With the five schools that I was invited to serve, I would be neither of the schools nor of the school districts, neither of the local reform movement nor of the national reform movement, neither a university employee nor a freelance consultant. In this intermediary zone, I was positioned somewhat "betwixt and between" all of these groups.

In spite of this apparent ambiguity, there was one aspect of my intermediary position that was a given. From both a research and a practice perspective, mine was an "agent central" role. I would interact collaboratively with other change agents—educators, students, community members, reform movement representatives, and formal evaluation team members (who would be appointed later)—whose roles and tasks meshed with mine in various ways. In the intermediary zone, "commonplaces of experience" (Lane, 1988) would bind us together in such a way that inquiry and generative change could be mingled. With Dewey's conceptualization of knowledge (1916, 1938) sitting at the heart of our middle-ground interactions, "the negotiation of shared meaning—aimed at more academically rich and purposeful action on behalf of students" (my letter to the schools, October 1998) formed the primary task in which we would engage.

UNCERTAIN BEGINNINGS

A week before the 1997–1998 school year ended, I was asked to attend a meeting at the local reform office. I imagined this might be an informational gathering where I would meet the school-based educators as well as other planning and evaluation consultants, mostly professors from other local universities. The meeting, however, took an unexpected turn. A planning and evaluation template was introduced, not as an exploratory model about which opinions were sought, but as an instrument that the schools were expected to complete for funding purposes. As planning and evaluation consultants, we were informed that our function was to help the school teams (faculty and influential community members) complete the form during a 2-day retreat the following week.

Unfortunately, the instrument embodied the reservations held by the school-based educators. What was thought to be a leading edge approach, the principals viewed as "the same old, tired method"; what was understood to be a consultative manner, the school people experienced as an attempted act of collusion; what were considered figurehead academic positions, the university-based change agents interpreted as active advisory roles. On this occasion, the broad range of opinions held by change agents involved in the same reform initiative first bubbled to the surface. At this time, different views concerning the substance and process of change became apparent.

The Planning and Evaluation Retreat

The day after school officially ended, the retreat occurred. Looking worn-out and in serious need of vacation, the principal and teacher change agents from the 11 schools participating in the grant program assembled together with their planning and evaluation consultants and representative community members. From the outset, no one seemed happy about attending 2 days of meetings. None seemed thrilled about writing a "request for funding" proposal. Presenter after presenter, representing both local universities and school districts, made informal speeches to the school-based change agents who sat quietly in the audience. In the presentations, some speakers focused entirely on students, teachers, and schools; others paid close attention to the preparation of documents that would satisfy particular sectors of the community; still others emphasized how to "ready up" data so that it would be easily accessible to the external evaluator who had not been identified. Despite an obvious commitment to school reform, marked differences of opinion again arose between and among change agents.

When the scheduled time for school teams to work together came, I requested a space for the five teams with whom I had been working. My intent was to give us a place and room to talk frankly with one another. We gathered with the community leaders in an amphitheater down the hall. I sat in the background, listening intently, while the school-based educators began to voice their disappointment over what had taken place thus far in the retreat. One principal, for example, expressed his concern that schools that had been publicly recognized as successes were not being listened to as he had anticipated—this was supposed to be a collaboration after all! A second administrator took the position that reform automatically "implies that evaluation will be done differently," and a third principal spoke of the emergence of a whole new set of challenges. Teacher change agents from the schools also joined the discussion. They expressed the frustration about giving up the first 2 days of vacation "to be talked at." They claimed this was "valuable time" that could have been used in many other ways. The idea of some local change agents constraining the thoughts and activities of other local change agents surfaced. For all of us, the enormous complexity of trying to transform what had begun as homespun change in several isolated schools into a cohesive, organized reform presence that would serve all of our students and schools well became strikingly obvious.

The concerns of the educators in the group were noted and addressed by the African American, Latino, and White community representatives who were present. These were business people, church leaders, school district personnel, university professors, parents, and activists from all socioeconomic levels. They expressed their regret that the school-based change agents did not feel heard in the ways that they had hoped. They, too, had observations and advice to offer. One community leader summed up the discussion saying, "It is clear that you have not yet been able to spread your wings in the ways you know will work for you."

Important bonds were forged that day among the five schools, their change agent educators, their community advocates, and me. That day I consciously awakened to an understanding that had tacitly underpinned my beliefs and actions for some time: I recognized that what we were involved in was about something much larger than any of us individually or even all of us collectively. What we were doing was attempting to leave an educational legacy for present and future children that transcended socioeconomic, racial, cultural, and, for me, national, lines. I also realized, more clearly than ever before, how messy the practice of school reform is, and how limited both resources and rewards are even for those school-based change agents who are experiencing the most "success." I took comfort in the words of a wise teacher who quietly whispered to me in the middle of the discussions that there would be "gold stars in heaven" for those of us who were able to persevere and face the daunting challenges embedded in this urgently pressing and enormously interesting work.

In the end, the five teams, their supporters, and I left the retreat without written plans in hand. However, we departed with a solid cross-school commitment to work together to improve public education for all youth.

Postretreat Developments

In the aftermath of the retreat, I struggled to make sense of the events that had transpired. How and why did a group of people so collectively desirous of school change become divided over how the reform work would be planned and formatively evaluated? In my journal, I listed the issues that the retreat had brought to the surface:

- Need for documentation of some sort
- Desire for . . . direction [that is] open-ended
- Ongoing concern that school-based educators and other change agents will get caught "in the middle"
- Undercurrent regarding who owns and controls school reform efforts, particularly when not all change agents participate on the scene
- Unavoidable tensions that occur when those advocating for hard-sided approaches to school reform meet with those successfully living soft-sided approaches

Having lived a firsthand experience of the "the push and pull" forces of school reform, the school-based educators and I took a break. A healthy distance between the retreat experience and the collaborative planning sessions was needed. While on vacation, an informational message was received from the local office of the reform movement that gave the schools permission to plan "in their own ways." That communication was followed by a huge gulf of silence. The next news was that the local movement was without a leader, and that we were to continue with the planning, keeping the mission of the reform movement in mind.

BEGINNING AGAIN . . . OUR WAY

Freed from a template developed and determined by others and from a process that had regrettably become the antithesis of what participants and the reform movement both intended and expected, the school teams and I immersed ourselves in authentic planning. We particularly emphasized thoughtful actions that would expand our horizons of knowing and better serving urban youth.

Student-teacher relationships became the centerpiece of our individual and shared inquiries. Clean lines were intentionally kept between the reform plans and funding issues. The retreat experience dramatically reinforced this notion. Setting one's gaze solely on the budget, a particular sector of the community, or on the yet-to-be-named external evaluator, we had learned, would not serve the reform effort well. We needed to focus on developing practices and structures that would give rise to sustained change that would leave a lasting imprint on the educational enterprise (Cuban, 1990; Tyack & Cuban, 1995).

In the process, I interacted individually with each school, collaboratively with different configurations of schools, and frequently with all of them. I approached the educators in a consultative manner because I did not want to force the schools into collaboration with one another nor into isolated planning sessions with me. Work in the intermediary zone demanded this kind of close communication and shared decision making. If we were to have an enduring effect on schools or on how educators (as individuals) and schools and universities (as institutions) relate to one another, the ways we worked together would have to be informed by the wishes and desires of the people. Any other approach would be restrictive, limiting. At the same time, I admit to being hopeful that the collaborative plot line I lived in the intermediary zone would "rub off" on the campuses and school-based change agents.

Planning and Evaluation Meetings, Take Two

It goes without saying that the retreat formed a very real commonplace of experience that no change agents—principals, teachers, community members, and planning and evaluation consultants alike—wished to repeat. Even though the experiential tension arose from differing agendas with respect to how to approach and account for school change, the focal point for the individual and collective unease would always be attributed—in a misdirected way—to the reform movement. The task for those of us who continued in the intermediary work was one of acknowledging, re-storying, and attempting to relive that narrative history.

In the absence of an executive director, a very conscientious board representative responsible for evaluation met regularly with the planning and evaluation consultants from all of the schools in order to make sure that the site-based planning teams actively participated in the setting of agendas. In an effort to support the schools and secure the necessary funding, we all wanted to explore alternate approaches to planning and evaluation, particularly those outlined in the literature associated with the reform movement. After a few sessions where we focused on learning, it was agreed that Schön and McDonald's "theory of action" framework (1998) fit with the schools' preferences. As a planning and evaluation group, we pledged to work together as cohesively as possible in the intermediary zone to break down the sacred story (Clandinin & Connelly, 1995; Crites, 1979) of competition that seemed bred in our bones and lived out across universities and schools. And we recognized the need to consciously address the theory-practice split in our intermediary practices.

These were major leaps of faith for individuals who did not know each other particularly well. Individually and collectively, we awakened to the fact that, like it or not, we were the reform movement as far as the schools were concerned. The onus was placed on those of us positioned in the intermediary zone to figure out how to make things work. This was a responsibility that was taken very seriously.

School Reform Teams

At each school, a team was established. Each school team consisted of the principal and a group of teachers, all of whom were individually and collectively responsible for representing and reporting to their colleagues. When I became involved, Cochrane Academy had a strong team in place; Eagle High School had a team that was in an expansion phase; and Hardy Academy had a team that had recently disbanded. In an effort to protect faculty from additional work, the school administrations at Heights Community Learning Center and T. P. Yaeger Middle School were holding onto the reform effort until it became stabilized.

The notion of change agents exchanging ideas between, among, and within institutions enabling schools and people to grow, develop, and participate in powerful ways was one that to one extent or another each participant began to test. Without the creation of intentional spaces and places to meet and a catalyst to bring people together, these geographically close schools and change agents would have remained unknown to one another, and none could have realized the tremendous energy for change that grew out of these interpersonal and cross-school collaborations.

New Leadership

The principal of Cochrane Academy assumed the executive director position of the reform movement. The lead evaluator of the reform effort also was later named, and the formal evaluation plan was subsequently approved. Replacement principals were also appointed. With these developments, the school reform outlook brightened and became more stable for all of us. The remaining administrators in the principal evaluation group and I were able to share the narrative history of the group with the administrators new to the reform initiative. In this way, we were able to introduce them to an understanding of interschool collaboration, which one veteran principal aptly described as "all in the same chapter, but not on the same page." The new principal at Hardy Academy noted a shift in his leadership style from being a self-described "autocratic leader" to becoming "a leader among leaders." He claimed that his transformation was made possible by the reform team approach adopted in his school. He noted that he found that by sharing the leadership broadly, he and his faculty could "dig much deeper" in jointly satisfying ways. And he found that his school became a model that could assist other schools in the throes of leadership change. T. P. Yaeger Middle School, for instance, turned to the Hardy Academy example for advice during their leadership transition.

School Portfolio Work

In addition to the cross-school principal group and the reform teams at the five schools that have already been described, there was a portfolio group. These were teachers and administrators from each of the five schools with which I worked. The school portfolio group, like the other two groups, mirrored to a certain extent the racial diversity of the faculties of the five schools. From its inception, this group of change agents was charged with documenting school reform as lived at each school. They were also asked to help teacher colleagues and the schools as organizations gather and learn from the evidence collected (Craig, 2000). The origins of the group and the shared work are discussed in the following excerpt from one of our early conversations:

Cheryl: The five original principals were initially concerned that only
— one method would be used to talk about your school reform efforts. Some of you were at the meetings and the retreat. They felt the approach would not give a full portrayal of what your schools are all about, the dynamics and complexities of it all . . .

Yaeger teacher: I am familiar with that history, too.

Cheryl: And that is where the portfolio idea came from . . .

Yeager teacher: The development of school portfolios was in the principals' minds long before the reform movement began to talk about accountability.

Eagle teacher: It sounds like the principals were asking for what we needed rather than waiting to see what we would be given.

Working in the school portfolio group, the teachers from the different schools learned from each other as the following exchange demonstrates:

Hardy teacher: I do not know where I am going with this particular
    (portfolio) piece I am working on right now. . . . But sometimes
    reading and talking about other pieces helps . . .
Eagle teacher: Yes.
Hardy teacher: You know, it kind of keeps the portfolio work going.
    Group meetings have really provided me with a context where I
    can function well. Being around the work, seeing other entries be-
    ing brought in . . . seeing different things and really looking at
    how the portfolio work is being approached. . . . And it gives me
    courage to go on . . . to take the work this way or that way . . . to
    throw new ideas out there . . .
Cheryl: Yes. How we came up with these 2 days to work together
    arose from a suggestion made by a Yaeger Middle School teacher.
    She felt she learned so much more from being around the other
    people in the portfolio group.

As they came together, the teachers shared their understanding of
the history of the schools' involvement with one another in the reform
process. In doing so, they drew on the portfolio processes that other
schools developed to document their collective school activities.

In the communities of knowing that developed out of these interactions over portfolios, differences between and among change agents and
campuses faded as portfolio evidence and the sharing of interpretive
knowledge concerning the human experience of school reform became
the central topics of inquiry, discussion, and analysis.

Growing Into My Role

In the gaps between people leaving positions and other people being
appointed to positions, I found that my role expanded greatly. I was, it
seems, a thread of continuity during these multiple transitions for the
schools, faculties, and the reform movement. Increasingly, I found myself identified as various teachers' personal mentor, and increasingly, I
was involved in the writing of letters of support, and so on. I also was
invited into classrooms on a more regular basis and asked to more
meetings and celebrations, but this openness came gradually. Although
the teachers and principals from the five campuses seemed to accept
one another fairly quickly, they were not as easily accepting of me. This
point was voiced a year and a half into the planning and evaluation
work as the following excerpt from the conversation of the portfolio
group shows:

Cheryl: At one school (where I used to work), the group sometimes met before I arrived and decided, "This is what we are going to share with her today."

Yaeger teacher: Oh, my word.

1st Eagle teacher: That is so funny because that was my initial reaction to you—with us, too, it was like, she is "the man" and we need to be perfect for her.

Yaeger teacher: That is because you did not have her living in your school for over a year like we did. We never had that issue.

Cochrane teacher: And for Cochrane, we came to know her before the retreat. And we already knew we did not have to do that.

Cheryl: So this is what makes relationships interesting for all of us.

1st Eagle teacher: Well, I have written about this before. We are teachers; we are pleasers. And somebody who is above us, we want to show that we are wonderful, and what is wonderful makes us interesting. But it is not the full picture.

Cheryl: Point of clarification: I do not consider myself above you. I think we have knowledge of different kinds.

2nd Eagle teacher: But being at the university does that to you.

Cheryl: I guess it does.

Cochrane teacher: Yes it does.

2nd Eagle teacher: That is why you were chosen to work with us.

Whenever my spirit would wane or fatigue would set in, I would remind myself of the "higher cause," the work the school-based educators had achieved thus far, and the faith they had placed in me. I would also recall poignant tales of students—the story about an immigrant child waking up with a rat on her tummy or the one about a high school student who begged her teacher to adopt her because she had no guardian and her clothing was too small. In the most exhausting and exasperating of situations, thoughts and images such as these would return me to the intermediary zone work with renewed determination and added spunk.

CONCLUSION

In this chapter, I have shared experiences lived in the intermediary zone as I began my extended work as a planning and evaluation consultant to five schools involved in an organized reform movement. As I have unraveled the "change agent among change agents" text, issues and concerns initially experienced by the educators with whom I worked and the challenges faced by a change initiative attempting to establish itself in a reforming city were revealed.

To a large extent, these stories revolved around issues of trust. The retreat, for example, assumed almost mythic proportions in the reform stories because it had run counter not only to expectations but also to beliefs about teaching and learning. For those of us situated in the in-between places, this event quickly taught us that our work in the intermediary zone was first and foremost about developing trust. And, we learned, it would take time, and it would require that we be there—present, regularly and predictably, among those who participated, particularly the school-based educators *and* the local reform representatives.

After trust, the enduring dilemma regarding the place of experts and expertise in the educational enterprise was a second major issue that my colleagues and I in the intermediary zone had to address. Having the university as our base made it inevitable that we would be perceived as "experts" and that teachers and even principals might assume ours to be a directive rather than collaborative stance. For us too, it was a dilemma. On the one hand, I deliberately shy away from a "high ground of theory" position that risks "flights from the field" (Schwab, 1983). At the same time, I recognize that there are skills and knowledge that I have that can be useful to others as my work with the portfolio group illustrated. Thus the intermediary zone requires that change agents walk a fine line, demonstrating a simultaneous willingness and ability to listen and really hear as well as the capacity to intervene in knowing ways when appropriate and when specifically called upon.

Then there were my own feelings and perspectives. I had not anticipated that the in-between work would be so complex. For a person interested in narrative, as I am, there was much to consider. There were administrator narratives, teacher narratives, student narratives, and parent narratives, as well as the plot lines lived by those directly associated with the reform movement and other intermediaries charged to act on behalf of it and the other six lead schools. There were also the "ghost stories" (Connelly & Clandinin, 1999) lived by change agents who rarely, if ever, appeared on the scene, but whose spheres of influence were great.

In the midst of this amazing plethora of human intention and experience, I found myself trying to make sense of the day-to-day, personal, and site-specific situations with reference to a multiyear, multisite, national vision. In many ways, I found myself alone. The school-based teams had one another; the local and national reform representatives had their organizations and networks; I was, as I wrote earlier "betwixt and between." This is a difficult position to maintain. How does one judge the impact of intermediary work? My sense of both community and efficacy came over time from those with whom I interacted closely—school-based educators, other academics in a virtual form of community, some of the other planning and evaluation consultants, and some of the local reform representatives. Ultimately, however, the value of sustained work in the intermediary zone will be reflected in rich stories of teacher learning and student learning that become lived and told, and relived and retold, over time.

Acknowledgments. I want to acknowledge the centrality of the school-based educators' experiences that form the background of this work. I deeply appreciate the opportunity to work in a sustained manner with the faculty and administration of the five schools, with the representatives of the reform movement, with the other planning and evaluation consultants, and other participating school-based educators. Gratitude is also extended to the Brown Foundation, Inc., who supported this research.

REFERENCES

Clandinin, D. J., & Connelly, F. M. (1995). *Teachers' professional knowledge landscapes.* New York: Teachers College Press.

Clandinin, D. J., & Connelly, F. M. (1996). Teachers' professional knowledge landscapes: Teacher stories—Stories of teachers—School stories—Stories of school. *Educational Researcher, 25*(3), 24–30.

Connelly, F. M., & Clandinin, D. J. (1999). *Shaping a professional identity: Stories of educational practice.* New York: Teachers College Press.

Craig, C. J. (1995). Knowledge communities: A way of making sense of how beginning teachers come to know. *Curriculum Inquiry, 25*(2), 151–175.

Craig, C. J. (1998). The influence of context on one teacher's interpretative knowledge of team teaching. *Teaching and Teacher Education, 14*(4), 371–383.

Craig, C. J. (2000, January 14–15). *School portfolio making: Developing teacher knowledge through cultivating communities of knowing.* Paper presented at the Narrative and Portfolio Conference, Harvard University, Cambridge, MA.

Craig, C. J. (2001). The relationship between and among teachers' narrative knowledge, communities of knowing, and school reform: A case of "The Monkey's Paw." *Curriculum Inquiry, 31*(3).

Crites, S. (1979). The aesthetics of self-deception. *Soundings, 72,* 107–129.

Cuban, L. (1990). Reforming again, again, and again. *Educational Researcher, 19*(1), 3–13.

Dewey, J. (1916). *Democracy and education.* New York: Macmillan.

Dewey, J. (1938). *Experience and education.* New York: Macmillan.

Lane, B. (1988). *Landscapes of the sacred: Geography and narrative in American spirituality.* New York: Paulist Press.

Lincoln, Y., & Guba, E. (1989). *Fourth generation evaluation.* Newberry Park, CA: Sage.

Mishler, E. G. (1990). Validation in inquiry-guided research: The role of exemplars in narrative studies. *Harvard Educational Review, 60*(4), 415–442.

Schön, D. A., & McDonald, J. P. (1998). *Doing what you mean to do in school reform.* Providence, RI: Brown University.

Schwab, J. J. (1983). The practical 4: Something for curriculum professors to do. *Curriculum Inquiry, 13*(3), 239–265.

Tyack, D., & Cuban, L. (1995). *Tinkering toward utopia: A century of public school reform.* Cambridge, MA: Harvard University Press.

Chapter 7

The Promise of Partnership for Promoting Reform

Anna Ershler Richert, Pamela Stoddard, and Michael Kass

The past decade of school reform in this nation has yielded numerous and often conflicting ideas about how the work of reform ought to be conducted. We are told by some that reform needs to be a "bottom-up" enterprise, that is, that the initial effort needs to begin at the reform site with local initiative. We are coached that a grassroots beginning will help ensure "buy-in" of those for whom the reform has most immediate consequence. At the same time, we are cautioned by others not to rely on bottom-up initiatives, that bottom-up strategies fade as the reform work becomes more complex. For this reason, we are coached that "top-down" strategies are most important at the beginning to ensure adequate coordination and sustained support. Of course, over the years of reform efforts, the bottom-up/top-down controversy has been resolved; it is clear to most of us doing this work that a strategy that blends the two approaches promises the best results (Fullan, 1993; Schlectly, 1990).

While there are many conflicting notions about how school reform ought to proceed, the school reform community across the nation has generated a number of reform principles that are widely shared. One of those principles is the necessarily collaborative nature of school reform work. We all seem to agree that the work of reform is so complex and multifaceted that it cannot be done alone. Rather, it must be done in a collective manner that is often structured into partnership arrangements of one kind or another. These partnerships typically cross institutional boundaries and bring together such entities as schools and universities, or state reform initiative organizations with businesses and school districts. The actual arrangements of these partnerships take different forms as well and include a variety of participant stakeholders—teachers, parents, school administrators, local community members, students, university faculty, district personnel, and so forth.

However, while it is commonly agreed that partnerships provide a necessary structure for reform and that broad representation from and within the constituent groups is necessary for successful change work, how to accomplish this goal is less well understood. Simply gathering people at one place for a shared purpose is difficult enough. Beyond that, we are uncertain how to create an inclusive process within which the many different voices of those affected by reform can actually be heard. Nor are we clear on how to work across the differences that these constituencies bring to the work. For instance, we all recognize that parents of immigrant children hold important knowledge about their children and their culture that is vital for teachers and schools. But how to overcome the barriers of custom, language, and time that keep many parents away from school is unknown, in spite of how valuable their knowledge could be to the successful running of those institutions.

Similarly difficult are the conversations that need to be facilitated among school and reform constituencies who view both the reform process and intended outcomes differently—district personnel and union leaders, for example, or skeptical parent groups and enthusiastic pro-reform teachers. While it is unclear how to bring these groups to the table, into the process, and into partnership with one another, it is clear that coming together is vital for an informed reform process. The importance of partnership to the reform process, along with the challenges of creating and sustaining partnerships, is the focus of this chapter.

In our Bay Area School Reform Collaborative's School-University Partnership (SUP) project, partnership itself—the act of partnering across institutional and ideological boundaries—is central to our work. Our role as outside change agents focuses on supporting school-university partnerships, which we have organized into a network called the School-University Partnership Learning Community. Given our focus on partnering for reform, this chapter presents what we have learned about partnership work and how to support it for the purpose of school change. We draw on our experience over the past 2 years to examine partnership both as an ideological construct and as a programmatic structure designed to bring about and sustain reform in schools.

We will begin by addressing the idea of partnership as a structure for change and discuss how we have conceptualized partnering as a vehicle for learning that leads to reform. Following this, we will describe the partnership structures of our collaborative work, both the partnership arrangements themselves and the web of partnerships that sustain the work. In the third section, we will discuss the effect of partnering on our efforts at reform, drawing on various data sources to examine the experience of partnering as described to us by the participants in our project. We will also include our initial impressions of the effect of those experiences on the participants' growing capabilities to initiate and support change at their home sites. Our data sources include field notes from partnership meetings and events, interview and questionnaire data from partnership members, and partnership documents created as part of the work. Given our early findings about the relationship between partnering, adult learning, and reform, we will conclude by reflecting on the support role for partnerships that we have assumed as the centerpiece of our change agentry work.

PARTNERSHIP, LEARNING, AND PROMOTING REFORM

In our view, learning is at the heart of school reform. We believe that in order for reform to occur learning must be going on in all aspects and at all levels of the school community. As school people learn, their practice changes, and the institutions that house those practices change in turn. For example, as teachers learn new things about their students, they can construct new ways of teaching them. As administrators learn from teachers the new demands of practice, they can construct new ways to manage schools and support both teacher and student learning. As parents watch their children grow and engage in the world in new ways, they learn how to support them as well. As the adults in organizations learn, the organization itself has the capacity to change and grow, and so, in a way, an organization can learn as well (Senge, 1990). Even in higher education, there can be this kind of transformation: University faculty can learn from watching their student teachers learn to teach. Student teachers can learn from a reflective examination of their work and from the university faculty and other adults who assist them in learning how to reflect well.

An important goal of our school reform work is to turn our schools into learning organizations that promote and support the learning of children and adults. If a school (including a school of higher education) is a learning organization, it will have the capacity to change to meet the changing needs and demands of its constituents. Embedded in this idea of learning lies our hope for changing American education to teach our nation's youth more equitably and powerfully. Thus, for the purposes of our work in creating schools as learning contexts, we needed to ask ourselves: What contextual conditions are necessary for promoting the powerful learning needed to bring about changes in schools?

The Social Construction of Knowledge

An important aspect of learning is that it occurs in collaboration as people work together to make sense of their world and their experience. According to current ideas of constructivist learning theory, learning occurs when people encounter new ideas and experiences and have an opportunity to reflect on them for the purpose of enhancing their understanding by drawing on their existing knowledge and beliefs. In the process, the learners construct new knowledge. Furthermore, given the complexity of the world that school people encounter and its highly social and political nature, the learning that goes on in the schools is best accomplished not by individuals working in isolation from one another but rather by people working together. Thus knowledge not only is constructed, it is socially constructed (Airasian & Walsh, 1997; O'Laughlin, 1992; Prawat, 1992).

For example, when teachers talk about why certain children are slow to understand the concept of negative numbers in mathematics and those same teachers have an opportunity to share their ideas and experiences with colleagues or parents, they are engaged in professional learning. In the process they collectively construct new knowledge about how children learn math. In the best of all worlds, that knowledge will guide their future teaching practice. As school principals come together to discuss the impact of a new state initiative regarding bilingual education, they bring to bear what they know and have experienced in the past to grapple with the circumstances and happenings of the present. In this process, they, too, construct new knowledge. In this instance, the new knowledge the principals construct may be broad in scope and far-reaching in potential effect; it could include such things as bilingual education itself, the politics of state initiative for school reform, the technicalities of managing legislative change, and so forth.

Partnership: Its Value in the Process

Where, then, does partnering fit in? The value of partnering in learning becomes increasingly evident as we consider (1) the complexity of the processes of both schooling and school reform, (2) the complexity of the processes of knowledge construction itself (Airasian & Walsh, 1997), and (3) the reality of cognitive limits adult learners bring to the processes of trying to make sense of the social circumstances of their lives (Shulman & Carey, 1984; Wineburg & Grossman, 1998). New understandings of school life and practice can be more powerfully developed by partnerships of school people (teachers, school administrators, parents, university faculty, students, and others) who come together to collaborate in an examination of things as they are and a construction of images and plans for what they might become.

Learning and the Value of Multiple Perspectives

The challenge we faced at the outset of our project was this: How do we create and support partnerships that bring together multiple voices and promote thoughtful deliberation of school practice that leads to the construction of new knowledge and eventually the reform of schools? The School-University Partnership Initiative was designed to answer this question and to address the challenges outlined above. Since its inception, the Initiative provided an operating structure of nested partnerships designed to promote adult (professional) learning that would lead to changed practice and eventually both school and university reform. We based this model of change on the idea that reform could be initiated and sustained by partnerships of representative stakeholders convening for the purpose of learning about their work from one another through a problem-centered process of inquiry. The fundamental structure we employed was partnership; our role as change agents was to support those partnerships in their work.

THE CHANGE AGENT CHALLENGES

Given our notion that learning is at the heart of meaningful change in schools, we established a set of procedures to keep learning at the center of the partnership work and to support the partnerships as they moved from learning to action. The challenges to accomplishing those coupled goals of learning and action are many. Several emerge directly from the structure of partnering across institutional lines: how to capitalize on multiple perspectives for learning rather than fracture because of them; how to invest representatives of different stakeholder groups in the common work which they may consider to be outside their immediate institutional agendas; how to build equity in the partnership group so that no particular participant (for example, university participants) had greater power than the others in the partnership conversations. Beyond these process challenges are the pedagogical challenges of creating learning opportunities for the partnership members once they actually convene: how to facilitate productive learning conversations; how to structure new ways to reflect that lead to the possibility of new understandings; how to provide opportunities for people to practice moving from understanding to action in a safe and supported way; how to continually refresh the partnership work with new things to think about and new partners to think with.

To address these challenges we designed and implemented a number of strategies that focus our work as outside support providers. In the following paragraphs we will highlight four of the strategies that we consider most central to our efforts, based on our experience of working in this initiative to promote professional learning that leads to reform in schools. The selection also reflects the results of a formative evaluation of our work, which has provided direction for ongoing adjustments over time.

Strategy 1: Common Principles to Guide the Change Process

The first strategy of our approach was to establish a set of common guidelines. The need for common guidelines was sparked by one of the initial challenges we faced as outside support change agents: how to prompt the creation of partnerships that in their form would maximize investment, learning, and incorporation of multiple perspectives on the part of the very different institutions and individuals who would be involved.

We determined this first challenge to be one of structure or design. Our initial design question was how to facilitate partnership work that was more than just a "coming together," and work that was seen not as a mechanism to "fix schools," but instead as one that directed the work toward the development of all participants and their home institutions, including both schools and universities. Additionally, we wanted to provide opportunities for learning through multiple parallel conversations about the work.

The guidelines were developed by a group of school, university, and business leaders knowledgeable about school reform. In addition to pooling their collective knowledge and wisdom about change in universities and schools, they reviewed the literature on school-university partnerships with a special focus on professional learning and reform. From the work of this group we culled a set guidelines for the Initiative.

The guidelines formed the basis for partnership development and selection. They require partnerships to demonstrate the following:

- A shared vision of teaching and learning
- A focus on the continuum of professional development that entails placing professional learning at the center of reform
- A plan that builds on the strengths and weaknesses of schools and universities to renew both institutions
- A focus on inquiry
- A set of governance and financial structures to support the partnership

We intended that the guidelines would help equalize the partnership relationships by undoing traditional hierarchies and promoting shared responsibility for the work. Additionally, the guidelines helped the partnerships focus on the coupled goals of professional development and institutional renewal. These goals directed the partnership constituencies to improve all facets of teacher education as a method for school reform, and by focusing the work on renewing both institutions, they led everyone to think of their home institutions as places of change. Because partnerships were asked to build on the strengths and weaknesses of the institutions involved, partnerships had to consider ways to flatten existing hierarchies between and within institutions and to capitalize on different perspectives, talents, and expertise. The guidelines also encouraged partnerships to utilize a common process of inquiry and develop a shared vision of teaching and learning, thus moving the agenda toward common goals rather than competing outcomes.

Following the establishment of the guidelines, our challenge was to assist partnerships in designing plans for change that were both responsive to them and innovative and reflective of the unique institutions in their partnership groups. Our aim was to draw on the guidelines in a manner that would benefit the agendas of each organization and, at the same time, facilitate investment in the joint work. The common goals helped establish a shared set of commitments and lay the groundwork for collaborative learning. Eventually, they also provided a foundation for the larger learning community, which was made up of eight different partnership teams. Since the partnerships shared both goals and processes in common, they had compelling reasons for working and learning together. For example, all of the partnerships were committed to developing plans for supporting the entire continuum of professional development. Similarly, they were focused on developing the requisite knowledge, skills, and dispositions for assuming an inquiry stance toward their work. Our efforts to support the partnership reform work assumed new dimensions as it fanned out from individual partnership support to assist the partnerships in their efforts to support one another as the collective work of the larger community progressed.

Strategy 2: Nested Partnerships for Learning

The collective work of the larger learning community raises the second strategy we employed in this reform initiative: establishing multiple opportunities for new collaboration and growth. An early concern of ours was that as the partnerships developed, they could fall prey to the very traps that plagued the institutions involved: They might either gravitate uncritically toward a shared perspective or, on the other hand, be stymied by competing opinions. Either way, we anticipated that the partnerships would benefit from new perspectives on their work and new opportunities to construct knowledge in collaboration. Consequently, we designed three levels of partnerships with three different configurations of people at each level: (1) the school-university individual or working partnership, which includes one or more schools or districts and one university partner (eight total); (2) the critical colleagues partnership ("critical colleagueship"), which pairs two of the partnerships at the first level (four total); and (3) the partnership of partnerships, which brings together all of the partnerships into a large Learning Community. Our change agentry involves planning and support for the partnership-learning work on all three levels.

The broadest of these levels is that of the SUP Learning Community, which meets 4 times a year to work together across all the partnerships on the project of professional development and institutional change. We designed all facets of the SUP Learning Community to maximize professional development for its participants based on principles of learning through inquiry such as reflection, multiple perspectives, and collaborative problem solving. The SUP Learning Community reinforces a sense of "commonness," in that it is built on the common guidelines and goals, shared accountability, and common content. In our framing of this larger Learning Community we intentionally included the many educational institutions of the Bay Area irrespective of whether they had membership partnerships. In this way, we invited to our conversation unaffiliated members of the larger local education community such as scholars from universities of the region whose work is relevant to our reform effort. Several of these scholars attended our meetings and spoke about their research. These presentations generated considerable discussion and resulted in an enhanced knowledge base for the work of reform. They also provided the community an expanded sense of whose work it is to reform schools.

The critical colleagueship layer of partnering—the structure that partners two partnership teams—was added to the plan near the close of the first year of the Learning Community's work when we hypothesized that a focused sharing of experiences would help each partnership progress towards its own goals. Our intention was to create new opportunities for cross-partnership conversations that were both consistent and predictable. We also wanted to provide more opportunities for dialogue than was possible in our large group discussions. As the partnership colleagues began to know one another's work better over time, they developed the capacity to enhance the learning potential of their partners in extraordinary ways. (We discuss this finding about our work in the last section of the chapter.) This aspect of the partnering structure has resulted in the partnerships receiving intensive, personalized assistance with their own particular work and approach.

Strategy 3: Common Content

A third strategy involved establishing a point of common focus for our work at both the partnership and Learning Community levels. The need for a focus that transcended professional development and institutional reform came from the two-part question: Toward what are we directing our change efforts? Change for what? After much discussion about this question among the steering committee and others, we decided to establish equity in our schools as a common goal. Thus our collective answer to the question was "toward change that will result in equitable and excellent outcomes for all students." This common focus, and the change agent work to establish and sustain it, has proven to be some of the most important work that we have done together so far.

This commitment came about as we set out to plan the Learning Community activities and looked for common ground within the partnership work. Although the partnerships had the common framework of the guiding principles, they were taking quite different approaches to change. In order to understand those approaches, we had to become clear about the goals toward which those approaches were directed. Interestingly, in exploring those coupled questions of goals and approaches, we discovered that though the approaches were different, the goals of the partnerships seemed to have much in common. For example, several of the partnerships were focused on literacy with the goal of helping all children learn to read, write, and talk in powerful ways; others had embraced efficacy with literacy as the vehicle for helping all children learn. All eight partnerships were focused in some way on creating schools that would produce equitable and excellent outcomes for all children.

We began to frame the overarching goal of equity as we considered the collective goals of literacy and efficacy that motivated and organized the partnership work. In one way or another each partnership developed a professional development plan designed to build new understandings, changed practices, and changed institutional structures that would support equitable and excellent outcomes for all students. Establishing equity as an overarching goal brought the Learning Community together and established the need for working collectively to understand better what equity means and how our work can move us toward it. An important strategy of our work, therefore, was to conduct the inquiry that led to the common focus and to broaden and deepen it at the same time.

While our equity-based efforts occur in many different places within the Initiative, the most visible occur at the larger Learning Community level where speakers have presented research about historically underserved student populations and issues around closing the achievement gap. Reflection and dialogue about equity have expanded the learning at all levels—from the whole-group conversations of the Learning Community, to critical colleagueships, and partnership interactions themselves. This focus was intended not only to provide a sense of common purpose, but also to encourage cross-partnership dialogue centering around students and results, rather than strategies and institutional change as ends in themselves.

Strategy 4: Shared Accountability

Our accountability strategy, which we see as a fourth dimension of our change agent work, also reflects the guiding idea of learning as the centerpiece of the partnership processes. We asked each partnership to create an accountability and documentation plan as part of its membership in the learning community. They were to organize their plan around three domains: student learning, adult learning, and institutional learning. We directed partnerships to collect and analyze data as a means of assessing the impact of their partnership work in each of these three areas.

Embedded in this work was the idea that learning is central to reform: As important as is the impact (or lack of it) to our collective work, learning about why the work was successful or not is equally important. A significant part of our accountability is examining what we learn from our data-based inquiry that sustains the reform effort and enhances the equity agenda in schools.

In addition to placing shared learning at the heart of our account-ability strategy, we established several norms for actions that we hoped would result in increased capacity for conducting inquiry that leads to the construction of meaningful local knowledge, which would, in turn, be used to guide improved practice. Establishing norms is critical to this accountability approach. In this instance these norms included the following: (1) The partnerships would decide themselves what they need to know to advance their work most powerfully; (2) they would establish means for answering the questions they raise in a systematic manner that involves the collection and analysis of relevant data; and (3) they would prepare their findings to be presented to an audience of their peers (i.e., the Learning Community itself). Our strategy was to move the accountability processes away from traditional methods of collecting findings focused on successes, which are then reported to an outside unknown audience, and toward collecting and analyzing data that lead to authentic learning about the work. The findings of this inquiry are reported to an inside, well-known audience, in this case, members of the Learning Community itself and the communities of students and parents the partnership work was ultimately designed to serve.

We incorporated accountability into the Learning Community activities for several reasons. First, it was intended to facilitate cross-partnership interactions that were learning occasions centered on results rather than sharing occasions focused on activities. Structuring cross-partnership discussion about data would augment the more casual encounters within critical colleagueships. Second, the accountability process meant that partnerships could make sense together of puzzling results and strengthen new plans for action by bringing multiple perspectives to bear on the issues. Because we launched the critical colleagueships long before dialogues around accountability, critical colleagues served as a more informed and committed audience for the inquiry work. The accountability work was intended to reinforce the guidelines in a way that was embedded in the work of the partnerships and strengthened it in ways that an add-on, such as a series of workshops, could not. Each partnership is engaged in data-based inquiry at the partnership level and is examining its work with regard to the guiding principles. Third, the accountability process meant that the partnerships had one additional common experience to facilitate their learning together. Because the partnerships are engaged in and examining different approaches to the work of reform, the accountability process pro-

vides an additional means to share results through a common framework.

Our role in this process was to establish and enact norms and processes to support the partnerships in their inquiry efforts. The goal was
to create the conditions whereby the accountability processes were
owned and valued by the partnership groups. We believe that only with
those matters in place does the accountability work become part of the
learning context it was designed to create.

WHAT WE'VE LEARNED ABOUT PARTNERING, LEARNING, AND REFORM

In this section we summarize our findings about the value of partnering
for learning that triggers and supports the development of a deeper
commitment to change. The data we have gathered about partnering in
different configurations—individual partnerships, critical colleagueships, and so forth—suggest that participants have begun to recognize
the importance of certain precursors to learning within a partnership
structure. Before seeing the value of coming together across institutional
lines (and often conflicting points of view), participants report that they
learned the importance of developing relationships with others with
whom they felt they had little in common. For example, one partnership
leader explained that one of the most difficult transitions in his partnership group was moving from a "defensive stance about one's own institutional programs" to an "explanatory stance about how the program
works, including its goals, accomplishments, and lessons learned." He
explained how partnering involved working to dislodge preconceptions
about the efforts of others, preconceptions which many times included
the tendency to blame others for the shortcomings of the schooling system: "Over time the process involved becoming open to better understanding the work and intentions of others," he explained.

Working together on challenging issues has been important to establishing these relationships and to understanding one another. Participants report that as they have partnered in addressing such issues, they
have seen how much they have in common with one another—clearly,
something they had not realized before the partnership work began. In
fact, as they have grown to understand one another, they have developed new shared understandings. As one participant described it, "The
more we grow together as a team, the more our philosophies merge
together." The data suggest that this understanding flows from genuine
connections that are made as people let their preconceived judgments

fall away. Participants report that these new nonjudgmental relationships leave them more open to considering new ideas and alternative ways of doing the work of school and school reform. They report being more open to speaking honestly with one another and to taking risks. As we know from learning theory, both honesty and risk taking are essential for learning and therefore an important outcome of the partnering strategies employed in this work.

Partnership and Possibility

Despite the early difficulties in establishing these new patterns of relating in open and honest ways across institutional lines, our data show that over time participants have come to value partnering as a way of doing their work and as essential to institutional change. Early in the process they recognized the limits of isolation. They report coming to view their partners as allies in the work of reforming schools. For instance, one principal explained how "involvement with [his] university partners gave [him] insight, knowledge, and collegial support to focus on student learning and effective teaching." He credits the partnership with helping him focus on specific goals and objectives for students that are based on inquiry and assessment.

While the partnership structure provides the opportunity for new relationships and a greater appreciation for the common ground partners share, it also provides the chance to appreciate and value important differences. The various configurations of partnership that the Initiative provides puts people in contact with one another in numerous ways, thus exposing them to many new ideas and multiple opportunities to practice the skill of conversation and learning across different points of view. As challenging as this work is (and as demanding as are the requirements for guidance and support), the benefits are not lost on the participants who comment frequently about what they learn from these experiences, not only about others, but also about themselves. Our data show unquestionably that the process of being exposed to and consideration of multiple points of view has provoked participants to reflect deeply about their personal practice and beliefs. One participant explained, "Exposure to different points of view has led to changes and modification of my opinions and ideas." Many teachers regularly report that involvement with the partnership has made them reflect more on their teaching; one remarked,

> I am not taking anything for granted any more, including my
> "tried and true" practices. I am more willing to read up on cur-

rent issues and research and, more important, make some effective changes in my instructional methods. Having the university staff on our campus has challenged me to look at what's going on, reflect on what I see, and attempt to make appropriate changes.

Another remarked that through interaction with others and testing her own beliefs and practices, she has deepened her understanding of the "reasons why" she is involved in education and what she needs to do "to be a better educator." Similarly, after discussions with members of other partnerships, a university participant stated the need to revisit her strategies and change how she worked with teacher candidates. Still other participants remarked that cross-partnership groupings resulted in new definitions for terms and ideas they thought they already understood. For instance one teacher reported expanding her conception of *equity* from "just being equal" to "a state of mind and a relationship between adults, students, community."

Networks and New Ideas

Participants in the Initiative consistently report a new awareness of the value of networking and problem solving with partnerships doing similar work. The data reveal participants becoming increasingly aware of the need to look beyond their own ranks for both ideas and feedback. They explain that although their individual partnerships already cross institutional lines, partners still tend to accommodate one another within their new groupings, which may cause their thinking to become "circular" or otherwise limited rather than visionary. Stepping outside of one's familiar ways of doing the work is both enlightening and renewing; they report that examining the work with "outsiders" creates opportunities for the generation of new ideas and enriched thinking on the part of individuals and partnerships alike. One partnership member described how having another partnership group to talk to helped him and his group clarify and articulate both what they were doing and why. Others report that the interactions have helped them develop a better understanding of how their activities are, and are not, addressing issues of equity.

Cross-partnership conversations offer fresh alternatives for practical day-to-day difficulties as well as exposure to new strategies. Partnership members explain that such exchanges give their teams new ideas that they discuss within their own partnerships, then embellish to create new knowledge for themselves about their work—student teacher/cooperating teacher seminars, in one instance, and a set of strategies to improve school image, in another. "Even if we don't use their ideas, we begin to think of alternatives," one explained.

> Each time we get together I learn more about our work, what we need to do next, and how to sustain the partnership. For example, we learned today that there are even more ways to assess student learning than we have envisioned, thanks to our critical colleagues.

Participants indicate that listening to the advice and experience of others has shaped and focused their work, and that they anticipate that this will continue through ongoing collaboration and discussions with other teams.

Dialogue and the Challenge of Change

We are learning from our data that this kind of insight is the product of dialogue among diverse practitioners. In the process of working in various partnership configurations, participants have had multiple opportunities to test and challenge their personal beliefs. These configurations and resulting dialogue are stimulating reflection and learning, but the resulting learning challenges are many. As one participant explained,

> The partnerships expand the resources, enlarge the learning community of the institutions involved, and in essence create a larger think tank. On the downside, there are challenges to what "I knew" and some struggle with a loss of control.

This temporary "loss of control," while indicative of the important disequilibrating stage of learning, is uncomfortable for all learners. It requires attention on the part of those in charge—the work needs to be supported consistently by the change-agent partner leaders. Providing support during this time of disequilibrium is especially important when learners come together from different places and do not have the safety of their home institutions to back them up.

Part of this disequilibrium or loss of control comes when participants encounter predictable conflicts as multiple points of view are expressed in learning conversations. Our data point to a growing realization on the part of participants that conflict is a natural part of this exchange and the learning that comes from it. Participants report a new awareness that working through the conflict leads to both compromise and new ways of thinking. They report learning that these changes, ultimately, result in more people sharing a stake in the work at hand. As one participant explained, the partnering experiences

> have really confirmed that we do need a level of provocation and argument to move forward. I've learned to not get threatened by stressful situations that arise within the partnership but rather to see them as part of the process of working together and that it is okay.

Differences as Opportunities for Change

Comments such as these reveal the shift we have observed from a view that differences in institutional perspective are a hindrance to change to one that appreciates difference as a fundamental condition for learning and growth. Similarly, such comments suggest that the partnerships have begun to find ways to surface multiple perspectives and incorporate them into decisions and activities. Some partnerships report beginning to realize how much can be gained from soliciting more voices in the process of reform. They have discussed mechanisms to put this in place at their home sites. For example, one participant commented,

> I've learned a lot about equity from many different perspectives. I'll work on building structures that give voice to all staff. I'll try to take small steps to integrate conflicting thoughts.

Another participant explained that her group is working on a structure for increased voice among the faculty. In both cases, it is clear that participants have learned that inclusion and voice in the process itself is absolutely essential to successful (albeit challenging) efforts at reform.

An additional aspect of what brings about a sense of renewal comes in participants' seeing themselves reflected in the work of others. Many report feeling a sense of inspiration that comes from sharing ideas with people whose experiences are at once both similar and different. The partners commonly express feeling encouraged through the validation from other partners concerning the difficult choices they have made in their work, the systems they have established, the activities and goals that represent their best attempts. They explain that even seeing similarities in their struggles has been a boost; one participant remarked that "meeting with other people who have grappled with the same issues and won has been very inspiring."

Working with other partnerships as critical colleagues or in the larger Learning Community provided a glimpse of the light at the end of the tunnel, when certain groups of colleagues had accomplished what others were working toward. Seeing others succeed gives hope that success is possible. It is clear from our data that sharing experiences across all kinds of institutional boundaries renews motivation for participants immersed in the hard early work of reforming schools. As one participant explained, sharing common experiences, successes, and challenges "enlivened and deepened our partnership work."

Perceptions of Self and Changed Roles in Practice

As partners, and teachers in particular, work across institutional lines, they seem to inherit a different sense of their role in the workings of school. We are finding evidence, for example, that a number of teachers in the Learning Community have adjusted their view of themselves within a system that often seems unchangeable. Several remarked that they feel teachers need to be more "proactive" in creating and facilitating change within the system. One reflected further on how the typical response of teachers—and one that needs to change—includes "behaving as victims regarding state policy." The teacher who made this comment explained further,

> If I don't want to be a victim, I must assume my power in a responsible, sensitive way: to continue to speak up and question the status quo, to help reactivate an important committee, to be compassionate with my students but be tough academically and maintain high standards.

This determination by teachers to expand their leadership roles at their home sites is corroborated by several administrators who report a changing role for teachers as a result of their involvement with the partnership and Learning Community. Similarly, university participants report realizing their responsibility to take on a stronger advocate and, perhaps, leadership role, both with their partnerships and their home institutions, around equity issues including the diversity of candidates in teacher education programs and equitable support for all beginning teachers.

Not only have teachers begun to situate themselves differently within the system once they've interacted with partnerships, they perceive that they are more valued as they join partnerships and learn alongside university partners. At the same time, university partners report becoming clearer on the special expertise of their teacher colleagues. This is evidenced powerfully in one partnership, for example, where participants report that more value is being placed on the insights of cooperating teachers in the development of effective pre-service education.

IN SUMMARY

The age-old aphorism that "two heads are better than one" or the similar "what we can do together is far greater than we could do alone" is clearly borne out in the school reform work of the partnerships described in this chapter. What is also clear from our analysis is that one of the most powerful aspects of the partnership configuration is the opportunity for learning it provides the participants. Learning, however, is not a foregone conclusion of partnership work. In fact, we have come to believe that one of the barriers to reform is the obstacle to learning that typically exists when people come together across institutional and ideological boundaries without support for the exchange of ideas, perspectives, and beliefs. Since it would be impossible to change institutions (schools, universities, teacher preparation, district administration, and so forth) without active participation of the persons whose work is located there, supporting the learning together across those boundaries seems to be essential to the methodology of reform.

Our role as outside change agents, therefore, has been to support the work of reform by supporting opportunities for learning for the reformers. To accomplish that, we employed a series of strategies to help the partnerships learn together about the work of schools, teaching, and reform. We found considerable evidence in our data that learning became a centerpiece in the work of the partnerships in both a collective and personal way. We also found that the exchange of ideas, theories, and problems across individuals, schools, partnerships, and the region offered participants a forum not only for their own learning, but also valuable practice for stimulating similar conversations back at their home sites.

For many of the participants, these conversations about the inner workings and challenges of schooling that confront us in modern American life were the first they had ever had with colleagues—a sad indictment, indeed. At the same time, it is important to hear the value of the work as many participants explained how this work gave them an opportunity "to talk about the hard, deep issues [they] have wanted to talk about all of their professional lives, but didn't know how." After practicing in the safe setting, they reported feeling prepared to "go back to [their] schools and do the same work"—dialoguing with the rest of the school community about issues that matter for children.

In these ways, the data we have collected thus far point to the potential of partnering not only as a sustained learning experience for partnerships, but one whose effects will ripple within the institutions involved, and, one hopes, outside those institutions to our greater Bay Area region.

REFERENCES

Airasian, P. S., & Walsh, M. D. (1997). Constructivist cautions. *Phi Delta Kappan, 78*(6), 444–449.

Fullan, M. (1993). *Change forces: Probing the depths of educational reform.* London: Falmer Press.

O'Laughlin, M. (1992). Rethinking science education: Beyond Piagetian constructivism toward a sociocultural model of teaching and learning. *Journal of Research in Science Teaching, 29,* 792.

O'Neil, J. (1995, April). On schools as learning organizations: A Conversation with Peter Senge. *Educational Leadership, 1,* 20–23.

Prawat, R. S. (1992). Teachers' beliefs about teaching and learning: A constructivist perspective. *American Journal of Education, 100,* 354–395.

Sarason, S. (1990). *The predictable failure of educational reform.* San Francisco: Jossey-Bass.

Schlecty, P. (1990). *Schools for the twenty-first century.* San Francisco: Jossey-Bass.

Senge, P. (1990). *The fifth discipline.* New York: Doubleday.

Shulman, L. S., & Cary, N. B. (1984). Psychology and the limitations of individual rationality: Implications for the study of reasoning and civility. *Review of Educational Research, 54*(4), 501–524.

Wineburg, S., & Grossman, P. (1998). Creating a community of learners among high school teachers. *Phi Delta Kappan, 79*(5), 350–353.

Chapter 8

The Professional Lives of Change Agents: What They Do and What They Know

Ann Lieberman

Anyone who has ever been involved organizationally in creating, supporting, or facilitating change in schools knows how quickly one becomes enmeshed in a tangled set of relationships. Lacking knowledge about the complexities of the school culture and unprepared to deal with a bewildering variety of ad hoc situations as well as the consequences of the new programs that are being introduced, change agents often do not even know where to go for help or support when they need it. (As Donald Schön reminded us some years ago, professionals often learn what they are doing in the process of doing it.) The chapters in this book dramatically show such people getting caught up in change efforts, running into obstacles that frustrate their work and working out strategies that, at least in a number of cases, achieve success along the way. These narratives, ranging from preschool reform to school-university partnerships, give us an inside look at the practical, personal, and professional problems that arise as change agents work in different contexts to help bring about school improvement. Moreover, reading them from a perspective shaped by the experience and knowledge of those "who passed this way before" enables us to make the distinction between problems that are inherent to the position and problems that are contemporary or idiosyncratic. Increasing our knowledge of the professional roles and relationships enables us to better understand the work of change agents and the effects that this work has on their lives.

Since the 1950s, researchers have studied and written about the role of the change agent in improving schools (Havelock & Havelock, 1973; Miles, 1959; Sarason, 1972; Saxl, Miles, & Lieberman, 1990; Schön, 1991). In this period of increased attention to school improvement, resulting in great numbers of outside people coming into schools, new roles are proliferating. They are known by many titles including guide, mentor, change facilitator, liaison, site facilitator, and teacher of teachers. Whatever their name, they are confronted with the problem of being outsiders trying to change what goes on inside the school culture. Such roles have been with us for many decades but, with a few exceptions, they have not been written about in ways that describe both the conceptual complexity and the practical strategies that change agents use in their work.

LEARNING FROM THE PAST

In his classic book, *Learning to Work in Groups*, Miles (1959) called attention to the idea of *process analysis,* "the deceptively simple activity of talking directly about what is going on in the situation rather than staying on the official task." Understanding that change agents develop an awareness of a situation, notice large and small things, take account of differences, and become more knowledgeable about the need for open communication, they become, he wrote, "self analytic, developing a sort of sustained mindfulness" (p. 41).

Miles, Saxl, and Lieberman (1988) observed that even within the same improvement programs some change agents were very successful, while others failed. They followed 17 New York–based change agents in school improvement programs and found 18 "key" skills that distinguished the successful ones (see Saxl et al., 1990). Some skills were general: Good facilitators were without exception, effective interpersonally, competent in groups, knowledgeable about content and pedagogy, and well organized. They were also adept at developing social processes such as conflict mediation, collaboration, or open communication. One critical variable among all these "assisters" was the ability to develop trust and rapport with their clients. Success in an improvement effort appeared to hinge on the change agent's ability to develop strong, supportive relationships with the client, whether groups, individuals, or organizations. Without this trust, work on improvement was halted, diverted, and invariably contentious.

Seeking to understand how change agents think and reflect upon their work, Donald Schön described numerous efforts in which the changing character of the situations of practice created problems of "complexity, uncertainty, instability and uniqueness" (quoted in Lieberman, 1988, p. 240; Schön, 1991). This explains some of the uneasiness many of the authors describe in their cases. The ability to problem solve under such conditions is an important skill for those who undertake these change agent roles. Since some difficult situations only become evident as one engages in trying to solve problems that arise during efforts to improve practice, Schön called our attention to the necessity of reflecting on one's own practice in order to make sense of the mundane as well as strange and puzzling circumstances.

In *The Creation of Settings and the Future Societies* Sarason (1972) offered some important insights into the role of leadership in the creation of new projects. Sarason's ideas about the inevitable problems of leadership include the following:

- *The leader and the beginning context.* People come to a setting with conflicting ideas and values even if they agree with the focus of the project.
- *The leader's sense of privacy and superiority.* There is the expectation that a leader is supposed to be strong, knowledgeable, and without weakness—even though problems appear that may be difficult to solve.
- *The socialization of the leader.* The context as well as the conflicting ideas and values of the clients help shape what leaders can and cannot do.

His discussion about these common, yet rarely discussed, features of leadership helped to reveal the contradictions and tensions that change agents feel and why the role of a change agent in a new setting is always problematic.

THE CHALLENGES AND TENSIONS OF CHANGE AGENTS

The chapters in this book, written at a time when there is increased pressure for results and accountability in schools, suggest some new understandings. Because students over the past 2 decades have increasingly represented wider ranges of economic and cultural diversity, the pressures on schools to successfully accommodate to these new conditions have escalated. These pressures have resulted in an increased focus on teachers, their performance, and ways in which it can be improved. This, in turn, has led to a concentration on adult learning in general and teacher professional development in particular. Much of the recent research in this area suggests that teachers learn more when they are part of a professional community that provides choice, flexibility, and autonomy (Grossman & Wineburg, 2000; Lieberman, 1995; McLaughlin & Talbert, 1993; Putnam & Borko, 2000). The pressures on schools and teachers from parents, districts, and states and the awareness of the new knowledge about adult learning—and the need for time for adults to learn as well as teach—puts change agents in positions where they face a variety of tensions. These tensions, which demand constant negotiation, are written about in all the chapters in this book and appear to be an inevitable part of the lives of change agents.

Taking a Stance That Is Both Collegial and Authoritative

As Sarason told us decades ago, every group has expectations that the leader knows all the answers. But this puts the change agent in direct contradiction to his or her need to create a professional community where indigenous leadership is encouraged. This contradiction is exacerbated by the growing understanding that there is "inside" knowledge that members of racial, ethnic, and professional groups have that is important to the work of school improvement, as well as valuable "outside" knowledge that the change agent may want to impart. Negotiating this tension requires an awareness that building a community must involve the participants in helping to create their own improvement plans, while at the same time providing the knowledge and leadership to move the group forward.

Creating a Vision for the Project vs. Developing a Vision

Change agents, in order to gain commitment from their clients to participate in an improvement project, have to provide vision for the direction the project should take. Participants must, at some level, understand why they would want to involve themselves in yet another project, what interest it holds for them, what the incentives are to participate. At the same time it is important to realize that, to energize a group, the people in the group must become involved in the development of the ideas. This is perhaps the most difficult transaction for change agents to negotiate. They must excite their clients about the ideas they propose—whether it be helping their clients gain a larger voice, creating a collaborative group that proposes ways to work, participating in gaining greater expertise—while at the same time encouraging the group to participate in modifying and shaping the vision as their knowledge and trust grow from working together. The change agent's role is much like a teacher. She or he must make decisions about when to teach directly and when to let the participants shape the agenda, when to press forward or when to go on a detour, when to set deadlines or when to let the group have time to develop their work. And as the members of the group take responsibility for changing their own practices and reducing their dependence on the leader, the change agent must learn to accept this reduced role as a positive achievement.

Making Technical Improvements vs. Cultural Changes

In the current press for immediate achievement gains, change agents find themselves teaching technical skills to enhance the quality of teachers' repertoires. This is understandable and laudable. But given what is known about the culture of schools, the isolation that most teachers experience in their schools, the importance of encouragement and support from colleagues and leaders, and the necessity for time to study and reflect on their work, it is vitally important to understand that cultural change must be a part of any change that is expected to last. Along with good professional development, teachers must also have time to practice their newfound skills, try them out, make changes, and get support for continuing to hone these skills. This means that during the school week there needs to be provision for teachers to talk together, work together, and share their expertise. It also means that the school culture must be infused with the idea that learning for adults is as important as the learning provided for students. Technical improvements without the necessary changes in the school culture will fade away like the morning dew after the project is over.

Providing a Process That Leads to Results

In schools and politics emphasis is now being placed on results—often measured by standardized tests—without regard for the processes by which these results are gained. Change agents, who have to deal with the pressure of producing results, must find a process for getting there, and this process has to involve a progression of learning experiences. All this takes time. Sometimes they shortchange the process to get to the results quickly, forgetting that adults, like children, learn at different rates and in different ways. Negotiating these differences demands constant attention to both the process and the results.

Transmitting or Transacting the Teaching and Learning Process

At one level it is understood that people learn by being told what to do. But learning has many levels, and these include building on prior knowledge and learning by interacting with ideas, trying them out, analyzing them, and eventually, perhaps, incorporating them into ways of being and acting. As change agents discover, there are times to "tell" and times for people to engage with ideas. Those who tell all the time lose their audience, yet those that only engage people, without providing some kind of conceptual basis for learning, lose their clients too. Teaching is both transmitting and engaging in transactional learning. But the tough part is knowing when to do which. Varying the way teachers learn is as important for the adults as it is for their students. "To everything there is a season": there are times for listening, acting, and reflecting, and finding these times not only makes for more interesting teaching but for more lasting learning.

Learning from Experts vs. Learning from Experience

Change agents realize that learning comes from different places. Teachers learn through their experience as well as from experts. Yet school systems are often organized as if learning from experts is the only way to learn. Consequently, many teachers feel that what they know is not important or meaningful. But the flip side of the coin is problematic too. Some things that teachers learn is "miseducative," as Dewey warned us a long time ago. So it is important to find a process that allows teachers to talk about what they are doing in an open environment that encourages feedback and constructive critique of their work. In this way teachers' experience is honored but not reified. When teachers feel that their experience is legitimated, they are often more open to learning from experts and exploring knowledge from outside their classroom.

THE PROFESSIONAL KNOWLEDGE OF CHANGE AGENTS

The reform of schools has been a part of the landscape since public schools began in the United States. For 50 years change agents from both inside and outside the school have been involved in facilitating improvements in teaching practice. The power and importance of the chapters in this book is that one gets to understand the work of change agents and the roles they play in a variety of contexts. Common to all of them is the problem of finding ways to get inside the school culture while remaining somewhat independent of it. Reading about the tensions that arise as a result of these contradictory pressures helps us to understand how change agents deal with these pressures and why negotiating them is central to their work.

Successful change agents recognize that their ultimate goal is to work themselves out of a job by facilitating the growth of leadership in the groups that they have organized or led. They learn to be sensitive to the variety and complexity of different ethnic, racial, and class differences in order to further the work of building a professional community around the goals of their particular project. Their success in improving areas of practice is dependent first on their ability to understand what exists—to use what is valuable, to build upon it, and to change it as necessary. But cultural sensitivity is not enough. While change agents need to know how to build trust and organize, manage, and empower groups, they must also have a deep understanding of the project's content. Many projects falter when the leadership emphasizes process and ignores content. Both are necessary.

Perhaps the greatest paradox that successful change agents face is that while creating a community of teachers—with all the contradictions, stresses, and strains that are part of such an effort—they do not themselves belong to a community of their own. Since they are in positions where they are often at odds with other roles and relationships in the school system, they need the support that such a community could provide. Doing good but getting grief for it takes its emotional toll. The change agents in this book, by making public their struggles, the strategies that they use, and the conceptual knowledge that underlies their work, are not only making a significant contribution to the field of educational change and school improvement but perhaps to the creation of a community for themselves as well.

REFERENCES

Grossman, P., & Wineburg, S. (2000, April). *In pursuit of teacher community.* Paper delivered at the annual meeting of the American Educational Research Association, New Orleans.

Havelock, R. G., & Havelock, M. (1973). *Training for change agents: A guide to the design of training programs in education and other fields.* Ann Arbor, MI: University of Michigan, Institute for Social Research, Center for Research on Utilization of Scientific Knowledge.

Lieberman, A. (1995). Practices that support teacher development: Transforming conceptions of professional learning. *Phi Delta Kappan*, 76(8), 591–596.

Lieberman, A. (Ed.). (1988). *Building a professional culture in schools*. New York: Teachers College Press.

McLaughlin, M. W., & Talbert, J. (1993). *Contexts that matter for teaching and learning*. Stanford, CA: Context Center for Teaching and Learning in Secondary Schools.

Miles, M. B. (1959). *Learning to work in groups*. New York: Teachers College Press.

Miles, M. B. (1998). Finding keys to school change: A 40-year odyssey. In A. Hargreaves, A. Lieberman, M. Fullan, & D. Hopkins (Eds.), *International handbook of educational change* (Vol. 1, pp. 37–69). London: Kluwer.

Miles, M. B., Saxl, E. R., & Lieberman, A. (1988). What skills do educational "change agents" need? An empirical view. *Curriculum Inquiry*, 18(2), 157–193.

Putnam, R. T., & Borko, H. (2000). What do new views of knowledge and thinking have to say about research on teacher learning? *Educational Researcher*, 29(1), 4–15.

Sarason, S. B. (1972). *The creation of settings and the future societies*. San Francisco: Jossey-Bass.

Saxl, E. R., Miles, M. B., & Lieberman, A. (1990). *Assisting change in education: A training program for school improvement facilitators*. Alexandria, VA: Association for Supervision and Curriculum Development.

Schön, D. A. (Ed.). (1991). *The reflective turn*. New York: Teachers College Press.

Odyssey of a Coach (In Process)

Charlotte Lak

The first thing I noticed
at this school
were the stairs,
9, 10, 11 staircases
(depending on how you count)
any one of which will
get you where you need to be
   (some more efficiently than others).

The main staircase splits in
two directions,
equidistant and sufficient to
reach the second floor, but
   separated by wide-open stairwells
on the way up
(a chasm crossed by a narrow bridge
at the summit).

My first steps at this school
were tentative,
unsteady,
reaching for safety,
   security,
   support.

This was a new position,
a new challenge,
an expectation for change
to be a literacy leader,
a guide.
And the school went in 9, 10, 11 different directions.

The principal sat
just to the left of center
as you entered the building
(and philosophically).
Her vision was strong,
    her focus, unwavering
        (at times unnerving),
for the restructuring task was
formidable and complex.

The first year was
trial by fire
trial and error
try it out
try again
trying
but satisfying.
And I learned which stairs led where.

Year 2
the bricks began to fall
—without warning—
from the facade of our building.
And our principal left
—without warning—
    in November.
And each of us
inside the building
came closer to the center,
seeking safety,
security, and
support.

Year 3 we watched
with anticipation

(and some trepidation)
as a new principal
walked in the door and
negotiated the
9, 10, 11 staircases
seeking the vision
   and focus
   misplaced
in our confusion.
And each of us did what was necessary
to stay centered.

My office now is
close to the center too.
And often, like
Grand Central Station,
a hub for exchange of
ideas, materials, and
ideals.

9, 10, 11 staircases
bring those from different directions
together.

About the Editors and the Contributors

Cheryl J. Craig is an associate professor in the Department of Curriculum and Instruction, School of Education, University of Houston. Craig's research has appeared in *Curriculum Inquiry, Journal of Curriculum and Supervision, Teaching and Teacher Education*, and in other journals and books. She completed her doctorate at the University of Alberta.

Marianne D'Emidio-Caston is a core faculty member in the MA in Education and Teacher Credential Program at Antioch University, Santa Barbara. She is also a senior researcher with the Center for Education and Development in Berkeley, California. Her co-authored study, "Making Meaning in Classrooms: An Investigation of Cognitive Processes in Aspiring Teachers, Experienced Teachers and Their Peers," won Distinguished Research in Teaching Award from the Association of Teacher Educators in 1995.

Margot Ely is an ethnographer of the classroom and a professor of Education at New York University. Her particular interests are qualitative research and the study of how people develop as reflective teachers and learners. Recent publications include *On Writing Qualitative Research: Living by Words* (Falmer, 1997), which she wrote with Ruth Vinz, Maryann Downing, and Margaret Anzul.

Anna Ershler Richert is the Sarlo Professor of Education at Mills College in Oakland, California, where she co-directs the Teachers for Tomorrow's Schools Credential and M.A. programs. Her current research occurs at the intersection of teacher learning and school reform. Her recent publications include the chapter "Narratives as Experience Texts: Writing Themselves Back In" from the forthcoming book *Teachers Caught in the Action: Professional Development That Matters*, edited by Ann Lieberman and Lynne Miller (Teachers College Press, 2001).

Helen Freidus is currently co-director of the Reading and Literacy Program at Bank Street College of Education, where she has been a faculty member since 1991. From 1996–1999, she served as a Principal Investigator for a 3-year OERI-funded study on the implementation of First Steps, an integrated approach to literacy in an urban school district. Prior to that, she served on the faculties of Teachers College, Columbia University, Manhattanville College, and Long Island University. Her most recent publications include "Teachers and Teacher Educators Talking Together" in *Revisiting a Progressive Pedagogy: The Developmental-Interaction Approach*, Nancy Nager & Edna K. Shapiro (Eds.) (SUNY Press, 1999), and "Mentoring Portfolio Development," in *With Portfolio in Hand: Portfolios in Teaching and Teacher* education, Nona Lyons (Ed.) (Teachers College Press, 1998).

Claudia Grose is a member of the graduate faculty at Lesley University's School of Education in Cambridge, Massachusetts. Recent publications include " 'I know English So Many, Mrs. Abbott:' Reciprocal Discoveries in a Linguistically Diverse Classroom" with S. Abbott (1998) in *Language Arts*, (75) 3, and other contributions to the field.

Kim Grose is the founder and former co-director of Partners in School Innovation. In 2000 she joined the San Francisco Organizing Project as a community organizer, developing community leaders to take action on issues of healthcare, housing, and education. She holds a B.A. degree in Anthropology from Stanford University and an M.Phil in Social Anthrolopogy from Oxford University, where she studied as a Rhodes Scholar.

Michael Kass is director of the Teacher Quality Collaboratory of the 21st Century Education Initiative at Joint Venture: Silicon Valley Network. He is on loan from the Palo Alto Unified School District, where he has served as an elementary school principal, kindergarten teacher, and high school teacher of theater. He received an B.A. in Russian from the University of Michigan, an M.A. in Russian Language and Literature from Stanford University, and an M.A. in Education (Administration and Policy Analysis), also from Stanford University.

Maris H. Krasnow is a clinical assistant professor of early childhood education in New York University's Department of Teaching and Learning. Dr. Krasnow's interests include school reform, curriculum design, teaching for social justice, and professional development. She received her doctorate from Teachers College, Columbia University.

Charlotte Lak is a staff developer with the Springfield, MA public schools. Most recently, she worked with teachers and researchers on the "First Steps" program. Poetry is a keen interest of hers, as is children's literature.

Ann Lieberman is a senior scholar at the Carnegie Foundation for the Advancement of Teaching and a visiting professor at Stanford University. She is an emeritus professor from Teachers College, Columbia University and former president of the American Educational Research Association (1992). Her latest book, edited with Lynne Miller, is *Teachers Caught in the Action: Professional Development That Matters* (Teachers College Press, 2001).

Cynthia McCallister, Ed.D., is an assistant professor of education in the Department of Teaching and Learning in the School of Education, New York University. She received her doctorate at the University of Maine. She conducts research on issues of school reform and literacy teaching and learning.

Margaret McNamara is the co-director of the Reading and Literacy Program at Bank Street College of Education. She holds a B.A. from Fordham University and an M.Ed. from Bank Street College.

LaMar Miller is a professor of education and executive director of the Metropolitan Center for Urban Education, New York University. His recent publications include *Brown v. the Board of Education: The Challenge for Today's Schools* (Teachers College Press, 1996), which he co-edited with Ellen Lagemann.

Frances Rust is associate professor and coordinator of Early Childhood and Elementary Education Curricula in the Department of Teaching and Learning at New York University. She is the winner of the 1985 AERA Outstanding Dissertation Award and recipient of the Teachers College Outstanding Alumni Award (1998). Her research and teaching focus is on teacher education and teacher research Her most recent books are *Changing Teaching, Changing Schools: Bringing Early Childhood Practice into Public Education* (1993, Teachers College Press) and *What Matters Most: Improving Student Achievement* (2000, NTPI), a volume of teacher research co-edited with Ellen Meyers as part of her work as advisor to the National Teacher Policy Institute.

Jon Snyder is the director of teacher education and a faculty member in the Graduate School of Education at the University of California at

Santa Barbara. He is also a Senior Researcher for the National Commission on Teaching and America's Future. He received his Ed.D. from Teachers College, Columbia University, where he was the associate director of Research for the National Center for the Restructuring of Education, Schools, and Teaching.

Pamela Stoddard is research and evaluation manager for the Bay Area School Reform Collaborative (BASRC), where she is engaged in research and evaluation in the areas of school/university partnerships, reform leadership, and district support for school change. She received a B.A. in English Literature from the University of California, Irvine, and an M.A. from University College, London, in Anglo-American Literary Relations.

Index